THE M & E H

Fina
Foreig

D P Whiting
M Tech, BSc (Econ), AIB, MInst AM

SIXTH EDITION

Pitman Publishing
128 Long Acre, London WC2E 9AN

First published 1966
Reprinted 1967
Second edition 1969
Reprinted 1970, 1971
Third edition 1973
Reprinted 1974, 1975
Fourth edition 1977
Reprinted 1979
Fifth edition 1981
Sixth edition 1986
Reprinted 1987

British Library Cataloguing in Publication Data

Whiting, D. P.
Finance of foreign trade.–6th ed.–(The
M & E handbook series, ISSN 0265-8828)
1. Commerce   2. Finance
I. Title
382   HF1008

ISBN 0-7121-0661-8

Founding Editor: P. W. D. Redmond

Printed and bound in Great Britain by
Richard Clay Ltd, Bungay, Suffolk

Preface

Britain must import goods in order to live, and to enable her to import she must also be able to sell her goods abroad. Foreign trade is therefore vital and it is important that as many people as possible, in industry and commerce, should understand the methods by which foreign trade is financed. This book is designed both to give the general reader a thorough grasp of these methods and to meet the requirements of students preparing for the Institute of Bankers' examination in Finance of International Trade. It meets the requirements of students studying the subject as part of a BTEC National or Higher National course, and is also intended for students studying Finance of International Trade for the Final Examination of the Institute of Freight Forwarders and for those students preparing for the International Trade and Payments examination of the Institute of Export.

This sixth edition has been produced at a time when the pound is floating and its value which rose on the strength of the UK's oil revenues has fallen back again. It has therefore been difficult to use exchange rate values that can be expected to be truly realistic during the foreseeable future. However, such changes as do occur should not destroy the usefulness of the arithmetic exchange rate examples given.

This new edition contains the English text of the 1983 revision of the Uniform Customs and Practice for Documentary Credits, which came into operation in October 1984.

Method of study. The student is advised to work through each part of the book in strict sequence. Read quickly through the text to get the broad picture of the contents and then, on reading a second time, do so in more detail, making sure that you understand each paragraph before passing on to the next. The student should then read the text a third time and memorise the essential facts.

Progress Tests. These tests are based on past examination questions and are meant for self-examination and revision. They are placed at the end of each chapter and should not be attempted until the chapter has been thoroughly learnt. Try to answer each question in full and then check your answer with the text (by means of the chapter and paragraph references printed after each question). Make frequent use of these tests as they are the best way of memorising the subject.

Test Papers and Examination Technique. At the end of the book are Appendixes of test papers and hints on examination technique. Do not attempt any of these test papers until you have mastered the hints on examination technique and have achieved complete confidence in answering the Progress Tests at the end of the relevant chapters.

When you attempt a test paper, do it under strict examination conditions and mark yourself by checking with the section references to the appropriate part of the text.

Acknowledgments. Copyright © in Appendix II: *Uniform Customs and Practice for Documentary Credits* (Publication No. 400) and Appendix III: *Uniform Rules for Collections* (Publication No. 322) is held by the International Chamber of Commerce, Paris. ICC publications are available from the ICC at 38 Cours Albert 1er, 75008 Paris, from the British National Committee of the ICC, Centre Point, 103 New Oxford Street, London WC1A 1QB, and from National Committees throughout the world. These Appendixes are reproduced by kind permission of the ICC. For further details of other ICC publications, see Appendix VII: Further reading.

1985

                                                    D P W

Contents

Part Two: THE FOREIGN EXCHANGE MARKET

Part Three: DEVELOPMENT OF OVERSEAS TRADE

List of Tables

PART ONE
FOREIGN TRADE

CHAPTER I

Background to Foreign Trade

IMPORTANCE OF FOREIGN TRADE

1. Britain's foreign trade position. Britain is an island of more than 50 million people, which has to import going on for half its food requirements and the major part of its raw materials. To import food she must export and to a considerable extent she sells manufactured goods overseas, which involves importing raw materials. This was the general picture until twenty to thirty years ago, i.e. importing food and raw materials and exporting manufactured goods, but since then our imports of manufactured goods have risen rapidly to the point where they are as much in terms of value as our exports of manufactured goods. In 1983 our imports of manufactured and semi-manufactured goods exceeded exports of such goods by £2,000 million.

A large part of world trade is still financed in sterling. It is thus desirable that the external value of the pound (the pound in terms of foreign currencies) should be maintained. This means that Britain must ensure that the costs and prices of her goods are kept in line with those of other countries so that she can sell her goods. Furthermore, the domestic demand for goods must be kept within bounds, so that goods for export are not deflected to the home market and imports do not become excessive.

2. The law of comparative costs. By specialising in the output of those goods in the production of which they have the comparative advantage (because, for instance, they are nearer the source of raw materials), countries can increase the total output of goods. However, such specialisation necessitates the exchange of goods between countries.

The following highly simplified example illustrates this economic law. By each using two units of economic resources, one in the production of each commodity, countries A and B produce the following quantities of potatoes and wheat.

1

	Potatoes	*Wheat*
Country A	10 units	3 units
Country B	4 units	11 units
	14 units	14 units

Country A obviously has the comparative advantage in the production of potatoes and country B has the advantage in the production of wheat. If they specialise (ignoring possible economies or diseconomies of increasing the scale of production) the outputs would be as follows.

Country A	20 units of potatoes
Country B	22 units of wheat

In reality, country A might well have the relative advantage in the production of both commodities, but would nevertheless find it worth while specialising in the commodity in which it had the greater advantage. The outputs of both commodities are increased and if they trade with one another both countries can consume more of both commodities, that is to say, their real national incomes will be increased.

3. Self-sufficiency. It is possible for a country to be self-sufficient using, for instance, artificial rubber instead of natural rubber if the latter cannot be produced at home. To be self-sufficient does deny a country, and other countries besides, the advantages of comparative costs being exploited to the full. Political barriers also make trading between some nations difficult, so that the full advantages of mutual trading are never achieved.

4. Capital investment. In trading with the rest of the world a country may export more than it imports. This enables the country concerned to send capital overseas for investment, and if capital is invested in the underdeveloped countries it is filling a vital need. Underdeveloped countries must obtain capital from overseas, as their living standards are too low for them to provide it themselves. Capital from overseas enables the less advanced nations to carry out capital expenditure projects, such as building power stations and carrying out irrigation schemes, which will increase their output of goods and services in the future and improve their living standards. As more prosperous communities, their demands for imported goods would then of course rise, and through the development of overseas trade their living standards, and those of other countries, would continuously improve.

THE GEOGRAPHICAL PATTERN OF TRADE

5. Trade with Europe. Since the mid-1960s there has been a dramatic change in the geographical distribution of both our imports and our exports. Even before we joined the European Economic Community our trade with Western Europe was increasing more rapidly than that with the rest of the world, but this growth was of course stimulated by our entry into the EEC.

The data in Table I show how between 1967 and 1984 the percentage of our total imports which came from the EEC rose from 27 per cent to 45 per cent and comparable figures in respect of our exports show a similar increase. These increases were mostly at the expense of our trade with North America and the other developed countries, the importance of which, in terms of the *share* of our trade, diminished.

TABLE I. THE GEOGRAPHICAL DISTRIBUTION OF TRADE

	1967(%)	1984(%)
UK imports from:		
EEC	27	45
Rest of Western Europe	13	12
North America	20	16
Other developed countries	10	5
Oil-exporting countries	9	8
Rest of the world	21	14
UK exports to:		
EEC	27	45
Rest of Western Europe	16	17
North America	16	14
Other developed countries	13	7
Oil-exporting countries	5	4
Rest of the world	22	13

BALANCE OF TRADE AND BALANCE OF PAYMENTS

6. The balance of trade. The difference between a country's imports of merchandise and its exports is called its balance of trade. Throughout the twentieth century up to 1980 Britain had an unfavourable balance of trade with the exception of the years 1956 and 1958. In 1980 the balance of trade swung very firmly in favour of Britain mostly as a result of our exports of North Sea oil but moved against us again in 1983 and 1984.

7. The balance of payments. An adverse balance of trade need not worry the country concerned if it is offset by a favourable balance in respect of its invisible trade. Whereas the balance of trade is concerned with trade in *goods* (visible trade), invisible trade is concerned with *services,* including banking, insurance and shipping services, and earnings from overseas investment (the provision of capital is a service for which Britain receives payment in the form of profits and dividends). The difference between a country's exports and imports of invisibles represents its net invisible earnings (assuming that exports exceed imports) and if these are added to the balance of trade the balance of payments on current account is arrived at.

In addition to the current balance of payments, account must be taken of the currency flow to arrive at the total of official financing necessary to balance the balance of payments overall. Before considering the overall position, Table II should be studied. This shows that in 1983 there was an adverse balance of trade amounting to £1,165 million which was fully offset by net invisible earnings, thus producing a favourable balance of payments on current account of £3,246 million. In 1984 the visible deficit was again offset by the invisible surplus, but the balance of payments surplus was very much reduced.

TABLE II. UK BALANCE OF TRADE AND PAYMENTS 1982-4
(Source: C.S.O. *Financial Statistics*)

	1982	£million 1983	1984
Visible balance	2,055	−1,165	−4,255
Interest, profits and dividends (net)	1,162	2,540	3,050
Services (net)	3,762	4,087	4,243
Transfers (net)	−2,056	−2,216	−2,414
Total invisibles (net)	2,868	4,411	4,879
Current balance	4,923	3,246	624

8. Capital account. A favourable balance of payments enables a country to export more capital overseas than is imported. There is usually a two-way traffic in capital; that is, a country will receive capital from overseas where, for instance, foreign companies are opening up subsidiary companies in that country, and the country will also send capital overseas. Every year, Britain invests a great deal of capital overseas, in addition to gifts (which are included in "invisibles"). Britain also imports capital when, for instance, an American corporation opens up a subsidiary company in Britain or buys up a British company. Account must also be taken of the currency transactions of the banks and the amount of import and export credit. This then leads to an overall position (*see* Table III) which has to be financed from official sources.

9. Financing the overall position. The government offsets the overall position by its transactions with the IMF and other monetary authorities, by foreign currency borrowing or by building up or depleting its reserves. Reference to Table III shows that in 1982 the favourable balance of payments on current account was more than offset by the outflow of capital from the UK. The authorities repaid some of the money previously borrowed from the IMF, but borrowed from other sources and reduced our foreign currency reserves by £1,421 million. In 1983 and 1984 further outflows occurred which exceeded the current balance of payments and to finance the overall deficits it was necessary to borrow in foreign currency and to deplete the reserves still further.

RECTIFYING A DEFICIT

10. Restricting imports. World trade is expanding year by year and a country might, therefore, quite reasonably expect a steady growth in both its imports and its exports. If imports increase more rapidly than exports, a balance of payments deficit on current account will be incurred and at first sight the most obvious thing to do to put matters right would appear to be to restrict imports. It must be remembered, however, that to restrict shipments from other countries will reduce their ability to buy our goods, which may well make the position worse in the long run.

If an analysis of imports shows that the growth was in shipments of raw materials, necessitated by expanding production of manufactured goods, then it may be wise to refrain from imposing controls of any kind, financing the deficit in the balance of payments by borrowing from overseas, in the hope that at least some of the increased production will be exported.

Even if the rapid growth in imports is attributable to greater imports of finished goods, the best action may not be to restrict them directly, especially as import controls bring retaliation. A better alternative might be to dampen down the excessive home demand for consumer goods (*see* **12** below).

TABLE III. UK BALANCE OF PAYMENTS 1982–4

	1982	*£million* 1983	1984
Current balance	4,923	3,246	624
Investment and other capital transactions:			
Official long-term capital	−337	−389	−407
Overseas investment in the United Kingdom	3,487	5,188	4,024
UK private investment overseas	−10,725	−11,580	−14,918
Overseas borrowing or lending (net) by UK banks and others	956	−502	2,423
Exchange reserves in sterling:			
British government stocks	−212	227	188
Banking and money market liabilities	438	786	1,089
Other external banking and money market liabilities in sterling	4,134	3,167	5,163
Trade credit	−1,385	−1,532	−451
Other transactions	252	−476	−398
Total investment and capital transactions	−3,392	−5,111	−3,287
Balancing item	−2,815	1,049	1,342
Allocation of Special Drawing Rights	—	—	—
Total affecting official financing *(including current balance)*	−1,284	−816	−1,321
Official financing:			
Net transactions with overseas monetary authorities	−163	−36	—
Foreign currency borrowing (net)	26	249	408
Official reserves (drawings on +, additions to −)	1,421	603	913
Total official financing	1,284	816	1,321

11. Obligations under GATT. Britain is a signatory of the General Agreement on Tariffs and Trade (GATT), designed to reduce trade barriers and bring about the maximum possible rate of growth in world trade. Under GATT, member countries have, by concerted action, reduced the level of tariffs between one another. On several occasions they have set about reducing tariffs by mutual agreement and have set themselves a target, i.e. 20 per cent, for the average level of reductions to be achieved. Once a country has reduced its tariffs in this way it cannot raise them without the agreement of the other GATT members. The 15 per cent surcharge on imports of manufactured and semi-manufactured goods, imposed by the government in 1964, was therefore contrary to both the letter and the spirit of the Agreement. It was, however, fairly generally accepted as necessary to overcome a balance of payments crisis, but only on condition that the surcharge was quickly removed, which was the case.

The GATT applies not only to tariffs, but also to quota restrictions and other import controls as well.

12. Monetary measures. If there is clear evidence of inflation, i.e. excessive purchasing power compared with the amount of goods and services available, and the excessive demand is causing imports to rise, there is a good case for using monetary measures to dampen down the demand. The use of such measures in this way has become generally known as a "credit squeeze". The monetary measures have included the following.

(*a*) *Interest rates.* By bringing about a rise in interest rates generally, money is made dearer to borrow and borrowing is discouraged. If interest rates are reduced, then borrowing is encouraged. Purchasing power is thus reduced or increased. For more than 270 years Bank Rate, the minimum rate of interest at which the Bank of England would discount first-class bills for the discount houses, was the predominant rate of interest and other rates changed up and down in association with it. In 1972 Bank Rate was replaced by Minimum Lending Rate, but this also has been placed in abeyance and instead the Bank of England has a number of interest rate bands, which are not published, but within which it will discount bills for the discount houses. It still has a powerful influence on interest rates in general through its activities in discounting bills and can quite effectively bring about an increase or a decrease in the rates.

Internationally, a change in interest rates in a financial centre such as London will either attract short-term capital from overseas or cause it to flow out of the country. An inflow of foreign currency into Britain brought about by higher interest rates helps to finance a balance of payments deficit, if there is one, and strengthens the value of sterling in terms of other currencies. This is partly because of the increased demand for sterling for investment purposes and partly because of the restoration of confidence in sterling resulting from the fact that Britain appears to be putting her house in order by dampening down domestic demand.

(b) *Open market operations.* By selling Treasury bills in the market, the Bank of England can "mop up" some of the excess of funds in the money market. Those institutions that buy the bills pay for them with cheques which reduce the banks' cash and force them to be restrictive in their attitude towards making advances and forcing up interest rates. The Bank of England can achieve the opposite effect by buying bills and thus increasing the supply of funds in the market and encouraging a downward movement in short-term interest rates.

(c) *Special deposits.* These are a set proportion of eligible liabilities which the banks are called upon to pay over to the Bank of England in cash. To do this may necessitate selling investments or restricting advances in order to maintain their reserve assets. However this measure has not been used since 1980, though the Bank has the power to reintroduce it at any time should it consider it necessary to do so.

(d) *Directives to the banks.* The Chancellor of the Exchequer can issue directives to the banks through the medium of the Bank of England, requesting them to adopt a restrictive policy concerning their advances generally, but to give priority to exporters. Since 1972 less use has been made of this method of control.

Up to 1980 the Chancellor of the Exchequer issued directives to the banks through the medium of the Bank of England, requiring them to restrict the level of their advances or to give priority to particular types of borrowers such as exporters. In the 1970s the directives were concerned also with the rate of growth of interest-bearing deposits. When the banks increased their deposits, and hence the money supply, by paying attractive rates of interest, they were penalised by the imposition of supplementary special deposits, on which no interest was paid if their deposits increased beyond a set limit.

(e) *Reserve ratios.* It is possible for a government or, if it has the powers, a central bank, to prescribe a minimum ratio to its liabilities which a bank must hold in certain liquid assets. By increasing the size of this requirement, the government could restrict the ability of the banks to increase their advances. A Reserve Ratio was imposed upon the British banks up to 1980, but since then there has been no such requirement. The banks and licensed deposit-takers are obliged to maintain a non-operational account balance at the Bank of England equal to one-half per cent of their eligible liabilities but this is not intended as a reserve requirement. The eligible banks must also lend a minimum of 2½ per cent of their eligible liabilities as call money to the discount houses on a daily basis and over a period of six months or a year this must average out at 4 per cent. Again the purpose of this is not to impose a reserve ratio but to ensure that the discount houses have adequate funds with which to maintain a sizeable market in bills through which the Bank of England can operate to influence interest rates.

Other monetary measures could include hire purchase restrictions, which would discourage the purchase of goods on credit, and raising the level of interest rates on National Savings to encourage saving and discourage spending.

13. Fiscal measures. Fiscal measures are concerned with a government's own revenue and expenditure; in other words they are techniques adopted by a government in its budgeting, designed to affect the level of economic activity in some way.

By deliberately budgeting to take more away from the community in taxation, a government can reduce the community's purchasing power, while if it reduces taxation the opposite effect is achieved. To help rectify a balance of payments deficit the first of these two alternatives would, of course, be used to dampen down the demand for goods.

Fiscal policy can also be aimed at stimulating particular industries such as those principally engaged in the export trade. For instance, financial assistance might be given to firms that open up new factories in areas of high unemployment, with priority being given to exporting firms.

By pruning its own expenditure during periods of credit restraint, the government can help to reduce the pressure of demand. This would apply directly in that the government would not be demanding as many goods and services for its own consumption and also indirectly because the banks cannot create credit unless there is a flow of new cash into the private sector of the community which would normally come from an increased amount of spending by the public sector.

14. Encouraging exports. Import controls, tariffs, monetary and fiscal measures are all, in the main, designed to stop or discourage imports. To rectify a balance of payments deficit it is desirable to try and narrow the gap from both sides, that is, to increase exports as well as to reduce imports. Part Three of this book deals in some detail with the measures that have been taken to boost Britain's export trade. The services available to the exporter are extensive and the development of these in the post-war years has greatly contributed to the expansion of Britain's overseas trade.

15. Devaluation. By reducing the official rate of exchange between its currency and other currencies or (under a system of floating exchange rates) allowing the value of its currency to fall, a country makes exports cheaper and so improves the balance of payments. If the value of the pound were to fall substantially an American trader would have an incentive to buy our goods because each £1 of sterling that he purchased in order to acquire our goods would cost him fewer dollars than before. Unfortunately, however, this is not the only effect. It also makes imports dearer in terms of sterling which, if raw materials and semimanufactures are imported, increases the cost of production and such an increase is bound to be reflected in export prices. Furthermore, in that domestic prices will be forced up, pressure for wage increases will mount to the extent that they are granted in excess of any increase in productivity and inflation will inevitably occur. It will also occur as the result of the fact that more goods will be exported and less imported. In other words, the supply of goods for domestic consumption will fall and incomes will exceed the supply of goods.

Incomes will, if anything, tend to rise at such a time because the export industries will be booming and workers in them working overtime. Strong disinflationary measures (*see* 12 and 13) would therefore have to be taken at the same time as the devaluation to counteract the highly inflationary effects of the measure. Under a system of floating exchange rates fluctuations should occur which in theory put the balance of payments right. An adverse balance of payments causes the value of sterling to depreciate to the point where our goods become cheaper and our exports are stimulated and the deficit is rectified. A surplus on the balance of payments causes the value of sterling to rise and our goods to become dearer, thus removing the surplus. However, the rate of exchange does not depend only on trade and thus the theory does not work so smoothly in practice.

16. An incomes policy. If incomes rise to a greater extent than the rate of increase in the output of goods, then inflation will occur. Inflation causes prices to rise and, as export prices cannot be divorced from domestic costs and prices, there is the danger of becoming less competitive overseas. A prices and incomes policy, if it succeeds in keeping incomes and production in equilibrium, is highly desirable from a balance of payments as well as a domestic point of view. Unfortunately, in that it is interfering with the market forces of supply and demand, an incomes policy creates an artificial situation which brings pressure for the restraint on incomes and prices to be removed. When it is removed there is then an upsurge in inflation.

PROGRESS TEST 1

1. Why is foreign trade so important to Britain?   **(1–3)**

2. Account for the changes in the geographical pattern of trade in recent years.   **(5)**

3. Distinguish between the balance of payments on current account and the overall balance   **(6, 9)**

4. What actions, concerning imports and exports, is a country likely to take when it incurs a persistent balance of payments deficit?   **(10, 11)**

5. Apart from controlling imports and encouraging exports, what alternative measures can be taken by a government to rectify a balance of payments deficit?   **(12–16)**

CHAPTER II

Methods of Settlement

USE OF THE BANKING SYSTEM

1. The banking system. When an importer buys goods from overseas, or an exporter sells goods, no movement of currencies from one country to another need be involved. Instead, transactions are settled through the banking system, which involves offsetting one debt against another. Each of the British banks has accounts with banks throughout the world in terms of the currencies of the countries concerned. At any one time, then, a British bank will have balances in each of the currencies in which foreign exchange transactions take place. Barclays Bank, for instance, will have US dollar balances at a number of banks dotted about the United States. Foreign banks, on the other hand, hold balances in sterling with the British banks so that at any particular time, reverting to the previous example, Barclays Bank may owe more to American banks than the American banks owe to Barclays, or vice versa.

An importer of goods who has a payment to make can do so in a variety of ways through the banking system, but whatever method is used, the effect will be to reduce the foreign currency balances of a British bank or to increase the sterling balances of a foreign bank. If, for instance, the customer asks his bank for a draft in dollars, this will be drawn on the bank's account at an American bank so that when the draft is eventually presented for payment at the American bank by the supplier of the goods the British bank's account will be debited. The British bank will have charged its customer in sterling for the draft at the appropriate rate of exchange at the time the draft was issued. A bank can replenish its stocks of foreign currencies by buying from its customers (such as exporters) claims against foreign banks and, if these are insufficient, can buy currencies in the foreign exchange market. A bank, or other foreign exchange dealer with, say, US dollar balances in excess of requirements, will be prepared to sell dollars to another dealer in need of them at the current market price for dollars. Throughout the day foreign currencies are bought and sold through the foreign exchange market. The operations of the foreign exchange market will be considered in greater detail in Part Two.

2. Nostro and vostro accounts. The accounts which a bank keeps with banks overseas are called its *nostro* (our) accounts and those accounts in its own books in the names of banks abroad are its *vostro* (your) accounts. If it requires a bank overseas, in France for instance, to make a payment it will send an instruction (by telegraphic means or by post—*see* **3** below) or by drawing a draft, instructing the bank to pay a sum in francs to a French beneficiary and to debit its nostro account. The British bank will keep a record of its nostro account (a mirror account as it is sometimes called) and this will be built into its accounting system, so that at any time it is aware of the balance outstanding on the account. If a transaction results in a foreign bank receiving a payment in sterling this will be credited by the British bank to the vostro account of the overseas bank. The reader will realise that this vostro account is a vostro account only as far as the British bank is concerned; to the foreign bank it is its nostro account. In trying to account for the bookkeeping transactions involved as a consequence of a payment through the banking system do not fall into the trap of thinking that if a nostro account is debited a vostro account is credited, for that would mean the payment will be made twice! If a bank instructs another bank to make a payment from its nostro account it (the British bank) will simply record the fact in its own record of that account.

3. Methods of payment. To the exporter of goods, the banking system offers several methods of receiving payment, and to the importer several ways of making payment. Two of these alternatives, *bills of exchange* and *documentary credits*, account for the major part of all international transactions and will, therefore, be dealt with in considerable detail in separate chapters of this book.

From the exporter's point of view the most satisfactory arrangement to ensure that the goods are paid for would be to receive payment in advance. While this might be practicable for small consignments sent overseas, such as postal packages sent to a large number of individual customers who have ordered goods in response to a mail order advertisement, it is hardly conceivable that many large orders between firms would be paid for in this way.

The next best thing is the *confirmed irrevocable documentary credit,* which ensures that the exporter receives payment immediately upon shipment, or within a stipulated time after shipment, provided that he has fulfilled all the requirements of the credit (*see* IV). After two firms have been trading with each other for some period of time and they have built up a relationship of trust, they may decide to change the system of settlement to that of documentary bills of exchange or clean bills of exchange (*see* III).

Other possibilities include the carrying out of transactions on *open account,* with the use of *telegraphic transfers, mail transfers, cheques* or *drafts* and SWIFT. These methods are described in sections **4–9**.

OPEN ACCOUNT AND REMITTANCES

4. Open account. Where the credit status and general reputation of the importer is high, the exporter may agree to supply his goods on an open account basis. By this it is meant that they would carry on their trade very much in the same way that they would if the two firms were both located in Britain. The exporter would despatch his goods, debiting his customer's account with their cost, and send the documents relating to the consignment direct to the importer. At some agreed period of time such as every month or three months, the importer would send a remittance to settle the outstanding balance on the open account. This settlement could, alternatively, take place at some agreed time after each shipment has been received.

5. Telegraphic transfers. The periodic settlement on an open account could be in the form of a telegraphic transfer. This is an instruction from the importer's bank to the exporter's bank (or some other bank in the exporter's country) to transfer some of the balance on its account to the person named in the transfer (the exporter). The importer must pay his bank the local currency equivalent of the sum in foreign currency that the correspondent bank hands over to the exporter. As the transfer is telegraphic this is the most speedy form of payment.

6. SWIFT. Transfers can also be made by the international tele-communications network set up by the Society for Worldwide Inter-bank Financial Telecommunications, which is largely replacing the telegraphic transfer system as far as transactions between the 700–800 member banks are concerned.

7. Mail transfer. This is similar to a telegraphic transfer except that the process takes longer because the advice to the correspondent bank is sent by mail and not telegraph.

8. Banker's draft. This is in effect a cheque drawn by one bank on another or by a bank upon itself. It can be drawn in the home currency or in a foreign currency. The exporter, on receiving the draft by post, would pay it into his bank account if it is in local currency or, if it is in sterling, sell it to his bank at the market rate for such drafts at the time.

9. Cheques. The importer might alternatively settle his account by drawing a cheque on his account with his bank and sending the cheque to the exporter. He would have to make sure, however, that in doing so he was not contravening the exchange control regulations of his country — there are now no exchange controls in the UK so that the use of cheques in this way is permissible. The exporter would then have to send the cheque to his bank for collection which would be both expensive and time consuming.

TRAVEL TRANSACTIONS

10. Foreign currency. When a customer goes abroad he may obtain foreign currency notes from his bank and also will take some sterling for use on the ship or aircraft if it is British. Some overseas countries impose a strict limit on the amount of their notes that may be taken into the country and the bank will advise on the amount that may be taken.

11. Traveller's cheques. The use of traveller's cheques is a convenient and safe way of providing for one's foreign currency needs when travelling. These can be in sterling or in foreign currency and either way will be cashed at a bank, or possibly a hotel or shop, in the country(ies) being visited to obtain local currency, or possibly to pay a bill. Usually a refund can be obtained, or the cheques replaced, if any are lost. The advantage of taking cheques denominated in foreign currency is that the rate of exchange is determined before the traveller goes abroad, whereas if traveller's cheques in sterling are taken the traveller must bear any exchange loss which occurs through a deterioration in the rate of exchange in the meantime. Traveller's cheques denominated in US dollars are commonly used when travelling to some parts of the world such as the West Indies.

12. Remittances and open credits. When a traveller knows that he will be located in a particular town for some time he may wish to have funds sent to a bank in that town by telegraphic transfer (TT), SWIFT or money transfer (MT) for him to collect at his convenience. Alternatively, he may ask his bank to arrange an open credit for him at the bank concerned in order that he may cash his own cheques up to an agreed amount. Either of these devices would be suitable also for someone who was going abroad to work for an extended period of time when he would wish to be able to draw some or all of his salary each month and, in the case of remittances set abroad, could arrange for an agreed sum to be sent each month.

13. Eurocheque cards. Banks will provide travellers with special cheque guarantee cards, usually valid for one year, against which their own cheques will be cashed at banks in Europe up to an agreed limit (at the time of writing £50 per cheque). In some cases a special type of cheque book is issued and the customer may not use his ordinary cheque book.

14. Credit cards. Access, Barclaycard and other credit cards may be used when buying goods at shops in most Continental countries on the same basis as in the UK and, similarly, cash may be drawn at banks up to certain limits.

15. Local accounts. Anyone who is going to be abroad for a lengthy period can ask his bank to arrange for an account to be opened for him with a local bank in the country concerned and for remittances to be sent for the credit of that account from time to time. The advantage of this is that he will be able to have a cheque book and to draw cheques denominated in the local currency and, possibly, have a cheque guarantee card which will make his cheques more acceptable in shops, hotels, etc.

A company sending a team of people abroad to construct a capital project may wish to have such an account opened through which the person in charge would be able to draw funds to pay wages and other expenditures and it may even be necessary for an overdraft limit to be arranged to meet a small subsidiary company's needs in the country concerned. This would be done by the parent company's bank in the UK which will give some form of undertaking to a correspondent bank to reimburse it, should the need arise, for any overdraft incurred up to an agreed limit.

PROGRESS TEST 2

1. What methods of payment are available to the importer? Which is the most satisfactory from his point of view? **(3)**

2. What is the difference between a nostro and a vostro account? **(2)**

3. What is meant by trading on open account? **(4)**

4. What are the advantages of using traveller's cheques when travelling abroad? **(11)**

5. Explain the difference between having funds remitted and having an open credit arranged for use when travelling abroad. **(12)**

6. What is the purpose of a Eurocheque card? **(13)**

7. May credit cards be used abroad? **(14)**

8. Under what circumstances might it be desirable to have a local bank account opened in a foreign country? **(15)**

9. How can a parent company arrange for a subsidiary company abroad to overdraw its local bank account? **(15)**

CHAPTER III

Terms of Delivery

EXPORT AND IMPORT PRICES

1. Price to the buyer. The price to the buyer overseas must depend upon who is to pay the various charges involved in transporting and insuring the goods, also the cost of obtaining some of the documents that the importer requires such as a consular invoice. The various ways of quoting the price so as to indicate who is to pay these charges are called *terms of delivery* and range from "ex works" at the one extreme to "franco domicile" at the other. These terms are dealt with in the following sections.

2. Ex works. This term means that the exporter is charging just the basic cost of the goods with the minimum of packaging and the buyer is responsible for the goods and for paying any expenses involved once they leave the factory gate. The exporter may well be asked to arrange for shipment and insurance of the goods and if this is so he will add the expenses involved to the ex works price, as they must be paid for by the buyer.

3. Free on rail (f.o.r.). This term includes the basic price of the goods plus the carriage of the goods to the railhead where delivery technically takes place. The buyer therefore is responsible for the goods once they have been delivered to the railway and he must pay the cost of transporting them by rail, insurance and any other expenses involved beyond that point.

4. Free alongside ship (f.a.s.). In addition to the basic price the exporter includes the cost of packaging and transportation to the docks or on to a lighter if the goods have to be taken out by lighter to the ship. The price does not include the charge for hauling the goods over the ship's rail and delivery takes place at the side of the ship.

5. Free on board (f.o.b.). Here the exporter is responsible for getting the goods over the ship's rail where delivery technically takes place. The usual practice is for the port at which the goods are to be loaded on board to be stated, such as "f.o.b. London". The price covers the basic cost of the goods plus all the expenses involved in getting the goods to the docks and on board the vessel. This will include the dock charges and port dues and loading charges, but the buyer is responsible for the freight charges from then on and takes delivery once the goods are over the ship's rail. He is also responsible for marine insurance.

6. Free carrier ... (named point). This term is used where the goods are being transported by such modern means of transport as containers and roll-on–roll-off transportation by lorries and trailers. The term is rather similar to f.o.b. but instead of discharging his responsibilities when he gets the goods over the ship's rail the exporter does so when he hands them over to the carrier at the named point. A carrier is a person or company which has undertaken to carry the goods by road, rail or air or a combination of these. This term of delivery and other more modern terms are reflected in the 1983 revision of *Uniform Customs and Practice for Documentary Credits* (*see* V).

7. Cost and freight (c. & f.). This term usually includes the port of destination such as "c. & f. Singapore". To the cost of the goods the exporter adds the costs involved in getting the goods to the port in the UK and on board the ship plus the cost of freight to the port of destination. The importer is responsible for cost of carriage from then on and for insuring the goods from the time they are loaded on board. Technical delivery takes place as the goods pass over the ship's rail.

8. Freight (or carriage) paid to ... (c.p.). This again is a relatively new term similar in effect to c. & f. but applying to multi-modal transport and containers. Ownership and risks are passed on when the goods are handed over to the carrier and carriage paid to the named point of destination.

9. Cost, insurance and freight (c.i.f.). This is a similar quotation to c. & f. but also includes the cost of marine insurance. Ownership is transferred when the goods pass over the ship's rail.

10. Freight (or carriage) and insurance paid to ... (c.i.p.). This term is very similar to c.i.f. and applies to goods handed over to a carrier for transportation to the point of destination. The cost of freight and insurance to that point is the responsibility of the exporter and title to the goods passes when they are handed over to the carrier.

11. Franco (or franco domicile). This term covers all the costs of freight, insurance, etc. right up to the point where the goods are delivered to the buyer's premises. Technical delivery, as well as actual delivery, takes place at these premises.

12. Other terms. The above sections cover only the most common terms of delivery but the reader will be able to understand such other terms as "ex warehouse" and "free on truck" from the terms already covered. The International Chamber of Commerce has produced a set of definitions called "Incoterms" which define the terms and the rights and obligations of the parties involved, and it is fairly common practice for the contract of sale between the exporter and the importer to include a reference to these terms so that in the event of any dispute they may be used to settle it.

PROGRESS TEST 3

1. Explain what is meant by the expression *terms of delivery*; why are they so important to both importers and exporters? **(1)**

2. Explain the term "ex works". Who is responsible for the costs of freight and insurance? **(2)**

3. When does technical delivery take place under an f.o.r. contract? **(3)**

4. With an f.a.s. contract who is responsible for the freight and insurance charges? **(4)**

5. When does delivery take place under an f.o.b. contract? **(5)**

6. What are the points of similarity between an f.o.b. and a Free Carrier ... (Named Point) contract? **(5, 6)**

7. Compare a c. & f. contract with a c.p. contract. **(7, 8)**

8. Under a c.i.f. contract who is responsible for the payment of freight and insurance charges? **(9)**

9. Compare a c.i.f. contract with a c.i.p. contract. **(9, 10)**

10. What is meant by franco domicile? **(11)**

11. What is the significance of the document called "Incoterms" to the buyer and seller? **(12)**

CHAPTER IV

Bills of Exchange

DEFINITION AND USE

1. Definition. A bill of exchange is defined in the Bills of Exchange Act 1882 as "an unconditional order in writing, addressed by one person to another, signed by the person giving it, requiring the person to whom it is addressed to pay on demand or at a fixed determinable future time a sum certain in money to, or to the order of, a specified person, or to bearer".

There are three main parties to a bill, the *drawer*, the *drawee* and the *payee*. The drawer is the person who draws the bill (i.e. the person to whom a debt is due). The drawee is the person to whom the bill is addressed and the payee is the person to whom the payment is to be made. Usually, though by no means always, the drawer and the payee are the same person or company. For an example of a bill of exchange, *see* Fig. 1. Both the drawer and the payee of the bill are Fabbrica Speciale S/A, an Italian firm which has exported a consignment of sparking plugs to Britain and is seeking reimbursement by drawing a 90-day sight bill under the documentary credit referred to in the bill. The drawee of this particular bill is Dogger Bank Ltd.

EXCHANGE FOR £1,000   15th February   19

At Ninety days after sight   *pay this* sole   *Bill of Exchange to the Order of*

ourselves

ONE THOUSAND POUNDS STERLING

in part utilisation of your irrevocable credit No. 935790

To Dogger Bank Ltd.,
Overseas Branch,
London.

For and on behalf of
Fabbrica Speciale S/A

....
Director

FIG. 1.   *A bill of exchange.*

2. The use of bills. The drawee's acceptance of a bill is necessary before he is legally liable thereon. Once the drawee has intimated his acceptance of the bill by writing his name across the face of it, i.e. he has become the acceptor of the bill, the trader who has supplied him with goods has a negotiable instrument which he can turn into cash immediately by negotiating it with his bank, if the bank is willing to do so. The exporter, who might otherwise have to wait for settlement some time after the goods have been received by the importer, can thus obtain payment quite soon after the goods have been shipped. The importer, on the other hand, if the bill is a usance bill payable, say, 60 or 90 days after sight, is given time in which to sell the goods and obtain the proceeds with which to meet the bill of exchange when it matures.

3. The due date. By virtue of the Banking and Financial Dealings Act 1971 three days of grace can no longer be added to the date of payment as fixed by a bill of exchange. A bill of exchange is therefore payable on the last day of the payment period unless that day is a Saturday, Sunday or bank holiday, in which case it is payable on the next working day. Where a bill is payable at a given number of months after sight, calendar months are used. A bill accepted on 20th March, payable three months after sight, would therefore be due for payment on 20th June. In computing the date of payment no allowance is made for any days lacking in a month, i.e. if during the usance of a bill there are some months with only 28, 29 or 30 days, then this makes no difference to the date of maturity. Therefore, if a three-month bill is dated 31st March it would be payable on 30th June and one dated 30th November would be due on 28th February, and 29th February in a leap year.

If a usance bill is expressed to be payable three months after date it is, of course, due three months after the actual date on the bill. If it is expressed to be payable three months after sight, on the other hand, maturity date is calculated from the date when the bill is presented to the drawee for acceptance, and as bills are normally accepted on the day they are presented for the purpose, the date of acceptance is usually taken as the date of sighting.

Where bills are payable at a number of days after date (or sight), say 60 days sight, then these days must be calculated precisely. For instance, a 60-day bill dated 29th June would be payable on 28th August.

4. Bills in a set. Bills of exchange are often drawn in sets of three. They are all identical apart from a reference to the other two, which usually takes the following form: "At 60 days sight pay this first bill of exchange (second unpaid)." If there is any delay in the receipt of the first copy of the bill, then the second copy can be presented. The drawee must, of course, ensure that he accepts only one copy of the bill.

LIABILITIES OF THE PARTIES

5. The drawer. Section 55 of the Bills of Exchange Act provides that in drawing a bill the drawer "engages that on due presentation it shall be accepted and paid according to its tenor and that if it be dishonoured he will compensate the holder or any endorser who is compelled to pay it, provided that the requisite proceedings on dishonour be duly taken". If a bank negotiates a bill of exchange for its customer it is protected by this section of the Act and has recourse against the drawer of the bill. Normally, however, a bank will require its customer to give it the additional protection of a signed undertaking that if the bill is unpaid he will repay the bank the sum advanced on the bill. The bank must make sure that the "requisite proceedings on dishonour" are taken.

6. Proceedings on dishonour.

(*a*)   *Notice of dishonour* must be given to the drawer and to each endorser against whom it is desirable to retain recourse.

(*b*)   *A foreign bill* dishonoured by non-acceptance must be duly *protested* for non-acceptance, and if such a bill is dishonoured by non-payment it must be duly protested for non-payment. Failure to protest releases the drawer and endorsers from liability on the bill.

In the United Kingdom a bill may be "*noted*" for non-acceptance or non-payment as a preliminary step to protesting. The formal procedure of protest provides proof of presentation and dishonour acceptable in a court of law. In some countries publicity is given to protested bills to discourage traders from dishonouring bills.

7. The acceptor. In accepting a bill of exchange, the acceptor undertakes that it will be paid within the terms of his acceptance. This applies whether or not he has received any consideration.

8. An endorser. A person who endorses a bill is liable on it to subsequent endorsers or holders of the bill. If, however, an endorser adds the words *sans recours* or *without recourse* after his signature, he limits his liability, but the holder of the bill has recourse to other parties to the bill whose liability has not been limited in this way.

TYPES OF BILL

9. Clean bills. Where the relations between the exporter and importer are long-standing, the exporter may be willing to send the documents direct to the importer and draw a clean bill (one without commercial documents attached—*see* **23** below), which he will pass to his bank for collection. This implies complete trust in the importer on the part of the exporter. Clean bills form only a small proportion of the bills used in international trade, but they are a cheap and convenient means of settlement where trade relations are sufficiently developed for goods to be supplied on open account and are a useful method of payment where goods are sent on consignment account to agents overseas. When a documentary bill is accepted and the documents handed over to the importer, the bill becomes a clean bill.

10. Documentary bills. Where a bill of exchange is accompanied by documents of title to goods it is called a documentary bill (*see* **23** below).

11. Short bills and long bills. A short bill is one which has only a few days to run to maturity, irrespective of the original tenor of the bill. The term "long bill" usually refers to bills having a usance of at least three months.

12. Bank bills. A bank bill is one which bears the acceptance of a bank. Such a bill carries little risk and can therefore be discounted at the finest rate, i.e. at the lowest rate of discount.

13. Trade bills. Bills drawn by and accepted by commercial firms are known as trade bills. Those bearing the signatures of firms of first-class repute are known as fine trade bills (or fine trade paper) and can be discounted at rates only fractionally higher than those for bank bills.

14. Accommodation bills. These are bills drawn as a means of enabling the drawer to raise funds. A person or company (such as a merchant bank) lends his or its name as drawee and acceptor of a bill to enable the drawer to raise funds by discounting the bill.

DOCUMENTARY BILLS

15. D/A and D/P bills. Documentary bills, as the name suggests, are bills which are accompanied by the documents of title to goods. The exporter sends his documents through his bank for delivery to the importer upon acceptance of the accompanying bill of exchange (D/A, i.e. documents against acceptance) or upon payment of the bill (D/P, i.e. documents upon payment). If the bill is a sight or demand bill, the documents will only be handed over against payment of the bill because acceptance is not involved. If the bill is a usance bill the documents are handed over against the drawee's acceptance of the bill if it is a D/A bill or against payment if it is a D/P bill, but in some instances, particularly in trade with the Far East, the documents may not be handed over until payment of the usance bill, even if it is a D/A bill. This often encourages the importer to pay the bill before maturity in order to obtain the documents. In some countries it is possible for the importer legally to demand the documents upon acceptance of the bill, even though the exporter's instructions are for documents against payment.

16. The documents. In drawing up their contract an exporter and an importer will agree upon the documents that are to accompany a documentary bill. In some cases the importer will have no choice but to ask for particular documents to comply with the laws and customs of his country. Usually these include several copies of the invoice, the bill of lading and the insurance policy or certificate, together with other documents such as a certificate of origin, a certificate of quality or a consular invoice. If the goods are despatched by rail or by air, then a railway receipt or air consignment note will be required instead of a bill of lading. Further comment on these documents is deferred to V, 7, where they are described in some detail in connection with documentary credits.

NEGOTIATION OF BILLS

17. Procedure. When a bank negotiates a bill of exchange and/or the shipping documents attached to it, it hands over the face value of the bill to its customer, less discount. This is a somewhat similar process to discounting a bill, but as far as foreign bills are concerned the practice is called *negotiation* and it usually involves more than the simple purchase of a bill. A bill may not in fact be involved in that it is not uncommon for a bank simply to buy the shipping documents. Where a bill is negotiated it is unlikely to have been accepted, whereas a bill that is discounted will have been accepted before being offered to a bank for discounting. A negotiated bill will not be rediscounted in the way that a discounted bill might be and it will not be held by the bank until maturity but sent off immediately for collection through a correspondent bank in the drawee's country. Whether a bill is discounted or negotiated the banker in effect advances the value of the bill to his customer until the proceeds are received, taking a small discount as commission. The banker has full recourse against the drawer (usually his customer) by virtue of s. 55 Bills of Exchange Act 1882 and, in addition, usually takes a signed undertaking from his customer that he will reimburse the bank in the event of the bill being dishonoured.

18. Additional security. In addition to the undertaking concerning dishonour, the bank may require the customer to sign an assignment giving a charge over any bills, and documents relating thereto, which the bank is collecting for the customer, or possibly over his book debts.

Furthermore, the bank may agree to negotiate a bill on the condition that the goods concerned have been covered by a policy issued by the Export Credits Guarantee Department, and that the benefits of the policy are assigned to the bank or that the guarantee is direct to the bank. An ECGD policy gives protection from the insolvency or protracted default in payment on the part of the importer or his refusal to take up the goods, and from the imposition of exchange control regulations in the importer's country which restrict the transfer of funds to Britain. These and other benefits under ECGD policies are dealt with more fully in XIII.

Having negotiated a bill, the bank becomes a *holder for value* and may secure the protection of being a *holder in due course,* which is defined in the Bills of Exchange Act as a holder of a bill "who takes it, complete and regular on the face of it and not overdue, in good faith, for valuable consideration and without knowledge of any defect in the title of the person from whom the bill was taken", thus obtaining a valid claim against all parties to the bill. The bank collects the proceeds on its own behalf.

If documents are attached to the bill which are to be handed over by a correspondent bank in the importer's country against acceptance of the bill (D/A) or upon payment (D/P), the bank will regard them as part of its security for the money advanced and will naturally take particular care to ensure that there are no discrepancies in the documents that will delay or prevent payment.

19. Advances against bills. When negotiating bills for its customer, a bank may not be prepared to advance the full amount; instead it may (and usually does) insist on retaining a "margin" which will be paid over to the customer when the bill is ultimately paid. The extent of the margin will, of course, depend upon the standing of the customer and the report (if one is obtained) on the standing of the drawee. It is normally about 10–15 per cent, but would be nil if the bank was covered by an ECGD bills guarantee.

20. Recourse. The negotiating bank has recourse against its customer and therefore depends in the last resort upon the standing of its customer.

BILLS FOR COLLECTION

21. Procedure. Where funds are not required immediately, or where bills are not sufficiently attractive to a banker for negotiation, they may be handed by an exporter to his bank for collection. The bank then acts merely as an agent for its customer, sending the bills (and documents if there are any) to a correspondent bank overseas, with a request that it presents the bills for acceptance (if necessary) and for payment, and that it remits the proceeds back to the exporter's bank.

In collecting a bill for a customer a bank simply acts on behalf of the customer, and, provided that the bank takes precise instructions from the customer and carries them out with care it is on reasonably safe ground. Since 1968 the British banks have adopted the *Uniform Rules for the Collection of Commercial Paper* (replaced by the *Uniform Rules for Collections* in 1979) drawn up by the International Chamber of Commerce, in conjunction with the banks. These *Uniform Rules* lay down the terms on which bills of exchange and other items are collected by the banks for their customers. The English text of the *Uniform Rules* is given in full in Appendix III and the most important aspects of the *Rules* are dealt with in 23 below.

22. The customer's instructions. When sending bills to a bank for collection the customer must give clear instructions on a number of points including those listed below, and the bank's instruction form will be so printed as to provide space for them. The form expressly states that the *Uniform Rules* will apply unless otherwise stated so that the *Rules* are in effect written into the bank's contract with its customer. The details on the form are transferred to the *Collection Order* which is sent with the bill for collection. Specific provisions are made to cover these and other points in the *Uniform Rules for Collections* (*see* **23**).

(*a*) *Documents against acceptance or payment.* If the bill is a usance bill, are the documents to be handed to the importer against acceptance or only on payment?

(*b*) *Dishonour.* What procedure is to be adopted in the event of dishonour? To whom should advice of dishonour be sent? Is the bill to be protested for non-acceptance and/or non-payment?

(*c*) *Storage and insurance.* In the event of dishonour, what steps are to be taken to store and insure the goods? The same problem arises where the goods arrive before the documents, and must also be provided for in the instructions. Where there is some delay in moving the goods from the port, a heavy demurrage charge may be incurred.

(*d*) *In case of need.* The exporter should state in his instructions whether there is some person to whom reference may be made in case of need. Precise instructions must be taken as to what the role of the "case of need" is to be. What authority is he to have to dispose of the goods on behalf of the exporter?

23. Uniform Rules for Collections. The *Uniform Rules for Collections* name five parties concerned with the collection of a bill as follows:

(*a*) the *customer* who as principal entrusts the collection of the bill to his bank;

(*b*) the *remitting bank* which is the bank collecting a bill for its customer;

(*c*) the *collecting bank* which is any bank other than the remitting bank involved in processing the collection order;

(*d*) the *presenting bank* which is the collecting bank that actually presents the bill to the drawee for acceptance and/or payment;

(*e*) the *drawee* who is the person specified as the one to whom the bill is to be presented.

The *Uniform Rules* distinguish between *commercial* documents and *financial* documents. The former are defined as invoices, shipping documents, documents of title or other similar documents, or any other documents whatsoever, not being financial documents. Financial documents are defined as bills of exchange, promissory notes, cheques, payment receipts or other similar instruments used for obtaining the payment of money. The distinction between the two types of documents is important in deciding which is a clean collection and which is a documentary collection. The former is concerned with the collection of financial documents while the latter is the collection of commercial documents with or without financial documents. Other points covered by the *Rules* are as follows:

(*a*) Banks must advise the party from whom the collection order is received if any documents are missing (Article 2).

(*b*) The collection order must bear the complete address of the drawee or of the domicile at which presentation is to be made (Article 8).

(*c*) Presentation for payment of sight drafts and of usance drafts for acceptance must be made without delay and usance drafts must be presented for payment not later than the maturity date (Article 9).

(*d*) The collection order must state D/A or D/P. In the absence of instructions documents will be released only against payment (Article 10).

(*e*) Partial payments of clean remittances may be accepted if the law in force in the place of payment permits this, and, in the case of documentary remittances, only if authorised in the collection order. The documents will only be released after final payment has been received (Article 13).

(*f*) The presenting bank is not responsible for the genuineness of the acceptor's signature (Article 15).

(*g*) The collection order must give specific instructions regarding protest for non-acceptance or non-payment and should clearly indicate the powers of a case-of-need (Articles 17, 18 and 19).

(*h*) Advice of payment or non-payment, acceptance or non-acceptance must be sent without delay and in the absence of instructions to the contrary, by the quickest mail (Article 20).

(*i*) If there is an unconditional and definitive interest clause in the financial document it can only be waived if the collection order permits. Interest not embodied in the financial document may be waived unless the collection order says otherwise (Article 21).

(*j*) If the drawee refuses to pay charges and expenses the commercial paper may be delivered without payment of them unless the collection order says otherwise (Article 22).

EXCHANGE CLAUSES

24. The purpose of an exchange clause. If a bill of exchange carries an exchange clause, it does so in order to establish the method of calculating the rate of exchange at which the bill is to be paid, so that dispute and uncertainty about the rate of exchange can be avoided.

Where an exporter has sold goods to, say, Italy and he draws a bill in Italian *lire,* he can avoid an exchange risk by selling the *lire* in the forward exchange market. If on the other hand he draws his bill for the sterling equivalent he should know in advance what amount he is to receive in his own currency, and, to make sure that he receives payment in full, he can insert an exchange clause on the face of the bill. If the clause so provides, he can ensure that bank charges by way of interest, commission, postages and stamp duty are met by the importer and not by himself and that there is no loss in exchange through the use of an unfavourable exchange rate.

25. Exchange as per endorsement. This type of clause is still commonly used on bills for negotiation drawn on Australia, South Africa and Zambia and usually takes the form of *Payable with exchange and stamps as per endorsement.* The purpose of the clause is to ensure that the importer pays an amount in his own currency which, when converted at the rate of exchange quoted in the endorsement, will be equivalent to the sterling amount of the bill.

The endorsed rate of exchange is inserted by the negotiating banker who, in fixing the rate, will charge interest to the date of maturity of the bill on the money that has been advanced to the exporter. It is the importer, therefore, who pays the interest charges and stamp duty. Furthermore, the importer also has no option as to the method of payment and cannot, therefore, find a cheaper way of remitting the sterling. It is for this reason that this type of clause is unpopular among importers.

Once a bill bearing the "Exchange as per endorsement" clause has been converted into the foreign currency, the amount of it is written on the face of the bill above the sterling amount and the bill becomes a foreign currency bill. The negotiating banker receives the amount in foreign currency when the bill matures, so that he has, in effect, bought the currency from his customer, paying the sterling amount for it. It is the banker who runs the exchange risk, but he covers himself by selling the currency forward.

An alternative clause for bills on Australia which are for negotiation is:

> *Payable at the Australian on London sight selling rate at the date of maturity, together with interest at . . . per cent per annum from the date of the draft to the approximate date of arrival of the proceeds in London, together with all bank charges and stamps.*

The effect of this clause is similar to that of the first type, in that the exporter receives the face value of the bill without any deductions for interest and other bank charges and stamp duty.

26. Australian bills for collection. The usual clause used on bills on Australia that are sent for collection is *Payable at the current rate of exchange for sight drafts on London plus stamp duty.*

The effect of this clause is that the exporter receives the face value of the bill less bank charges, which would include postage, unless the clause continued *and all bank charges and postage.*

27. The eastern clause. This clause is used on bills drawn on India, Pakistan and other eastern countries and is rather similar to the second clause referred to in **25** above. It is frequently referred to as the "interest clause". The clause, in addition to stipulating that the rate to be used is the correspondent bank's rate for demand drafts in London (the bank is named in the clause), provides that the bill is *Payable with interest at . . . per cent per annum from the date hereof until the approximate date of arrival of remittance in London.* The rate of interest for insertion in eastern clauses is fixed by the Eastern Exchange Banks' Association and there is a scale of commission and postal charges fixed by the Association.

28. Other clauses.

(*a*) *Payable without loss in exchange.*

(*b*) *Payable with approved banker's cheque on London for full face value.*

These two clauses ensure that the exporter receives the full sterling value of the bill, but allow the importer some flexibility as to the means of payment. The importer can accept the rate quoted by the collecting bank or alternatively obtain the remittance from some other bank.

The following clause, on the other hand, allows no such flexibility:

(c) *Payable at the collecting bank's selling rate for sight drafts* [or some other means of payment such as a mail transfer] *on London at the date of maturity.*

PROGRESS TEST 4

1. What is the purpose of drawing a bill of exchange on an importer? (**2**)

2. What is the due date of a three-months sight bill accepted on 19th June? When would a similar bill, accepted on 31st January, be due? (**3**)

3. When would a 90-day bill dated 29th April be due? (**3**)

4. What is meant by the dishonour of a bill and what is the procedure upon dishonour? (**5–6**)

5. Distinguish between D/P bills and D/A bills. (**15**)

6. Distinguish between negotiation and collection of a bill of exchange. What additional security might a bank require when negotiating a bill? (**17–20**)

7. What instructions will a bank require from its customer when collecting a bill of exchange? (**22**)

8. Distinguish between financial documents and commercial documents. (**23**)

9. Are partial payments allowed? (**23**)

10. Can interest charges be waived? (**23**)

11. What is the purpose of an "exchange as per endorsement" clause? (**25**)

12. What is the eastern clause? (**27**)

CHAPTER V

Documentary Credits

LETTERS OF CREDIT

1. Personal credits. A letter of credit may be a *personal credit* or a *commercial credit*. For the businessman or tourist travelling abroad the personal credit is a way of ensuring that he will be able to obtain money without delay, when he requires it, without having to carry a large amount of currency with him on his journey. It is a request in writing (usually, though not necessarily, from a bank), to a correspondent bank or agent to cash on demand any cheques, or drafts, drawn by the holder of the credit up to a limited amount. These credits may be drawn on particular correspondents or agents, in which case a specimen signature of the holder will be sent to the agents for comparison with that on the letter of credit.

Alternatively, personal credits may be *circular credits* or *worldwide credits* and be available for use at any of the issuing bank's agents in the countries covered by the credit. When such a credit is issued, the bank will supply the customer with a letter of identification bearing his signature and he must use this letter to identify himself when making use of the credit. Personal credits are no longer used extensively, there being more convenient and flexible ways of obtaining funds abroad such as travellers' cheques and cheques drawn against cheque guarantee cards (*see* II, **10–15**).

2. Commercial credits are letters addressed by a bank to a person or firm (the beneficiary) undertaking to permit the beneficiary to obtain money either immediately or within a set period, provided that the beneficiary fulfils the conditions laid down in the letter of credit. If the beneficiary is to obtain payment immediately, the credit is called a *sight credit* and if it is payable upon the maturity of a bill of exchange drawn under the terms of the credit, it is an *acceptance credit* or *term credit*. If it provides for the negotiation of a bill it is a *negotiation credit*.

Normally the beneficiary of a commercial credit is a seller of goods, who, once he has shipped his goods, can either obtain cash or draw a bill. If he is not required by the terms of the credit to present specified documents relating to the goods, the credit is called a *clean credit*.

Usually, however, the production of specified documents is necessary, in which case the credit is called a *documentary credit*.

THE DOCUMENTARY CREDIT

3. Uniform customs and practice. In 1963 the British banks put into force the *Uniform Customs and Practice for Documentary Credits* codified by the International Chamber of Commerce. Prior to that date the United Kingdom banks had remained aloof from the *Uniform Practice* despite its acceptance by a large number of nations since it was first drafted in 1933. New thinking about the code led to a thorough revision of it in 1963 into a form that was acceptable to British and Commonwealth banks. The *Uniform Customs and Practice* was subsequently revised again in 1974 and 1983, with Britain participating in its revision. The 1974 revision took into account the changes that had taken place in maritime transport, particularly containerisation and the development of combined transport. The 1983 revision takes into account further developments in this field and also pays particular attention to the introduction of new transport documents and new methods of producing them, as well as the use of electronic data processing for transmitting information. It also takes into account new types of documentary credit such as the deferred-payment credit and the stand-by credit. References are made to the English text of the code, where appropriate, in the following notes on documentary credits. The articles referred to in these notes are the articles of the *Uniform Customs and Practice (1983 Revision)*, which is printed in full in Appendix II.

4. Establishing the credit. Getting the buyer to open a documentary credit is the next best thing to obtaining a simple transfer of funds from the buyer of one's goods at some stage in the preparation and delivery of the shipment. The exporter, in specifying the method of payment in the contract for the goods, may stipulate that payment is to be made in this way. If the importer agrees with the terms of the contract, he will instruct his bank to open a documentary credit in favour of the exporter. In doing so, he will request his bank to stipulate in the credit all the documents which he requires the exporter to present before he receives payment for the goods (*see* Figs. 2 and 3). The importer's bank will draw up a letter of credit addressed to the seller of the goods and send it to a correspondent bank in the exporter's country (this correspondent bank need not be the exporter's own bank).

The correspondent bank will then, as requested, pass the letter of credit on to the exporter, acting simply as an agent for forwarding the letter and for paying cash or accepting bills as laid down in the credit. This bank will make it clear to the exporter that it is merely passing on

Metropolitan Bank Limited

Branch DOWNTOWN

Request to open
Documentary Credit

Date 2nd January

Please open for my/our account a Documentary Credit, in accordance with the undermentioned particulars.
I/We agree that, except so far as otherwise expressly stated, this Credit will be subject to the Uniform Customs
and Practice for Documentary Credits (1983 Revision), International Chamber of Commerce Publication No. 400
I/We undertake to execute (if not already executed) the Bank's usual Form of Indemnity

Signed Downtown Import Co. Ltd.

Entries must not be made in this margin	**When completing this form please follow carefully the general instructions overleaf.** *Delete as appropriate*
Type of credit	**Irrevocable** i.e. cannot be cancelled without beneficiaries' agreement ~~Revocable i.e. subject to cancellation~~
Method of advice	*airmail/*cable *full rate *full advice ~~cheapest rate~~ ~~brief details~~
Advising Bank Name and Address of beneficiary	*As far as possible this should be left to Metropolitan Bank Limited* Fabbrica Speciale, S/A, Milan
Amount	£ 100,000 say One Hundred Thousand Pounds
Availability	Valid until 31st March in Milan for *negotiation/~~acceptance/payment~~ *Enter date* *Enter place* This credit is available by drafts drawn at 90 days sight accompanied by the required documents
Documents required	Invoice *Full set shipped Bills of Lading to order and blank endorsed, marked *Freight paid/~~freight payable at destination~~ or ~~*Air Consignment Note~~ } evidencing goods addressed to; or } marked *Freight paid/~~freight payable~~ ~~*Combined Transport Document issued~~ at destination by _____ *Insurance *Policy/~~Certificate~~ for invoice amount plus 10 % covering Marine and War Risks and including other conditions and risks as follows _____ "theft, pilferage and non-delivery W.P.A." ~~*Insurance effected by _____ where no insurance is called for~~ **Other Documents** Certificate of Italian origin
Quantity & description of goods	200,000 SPARKING PLUGS
Price per unit *if any*	£ 0.50p
Terms & relative port or place	*C.I.F., ~~C & F, I.O.B., I A.S., F.O.R.~~, etc _____ *This information is required in all cases*
Despatch/Shipment	From Genoa to London Part Shipments *allowed/~~not allowed~~ Transhipment *allowed/~~not allowed~~
Documents to be presented	For *negotiation/~~acceptance/payment~~ within 90 days of the date of issue of the Bills of Lading or other shipping documents but in any event within the credit validity
Special instructions *if any*	No Special Instructions

FIG. 2. *Request form for opening a documentary credit.*

General instructions for opening Documentary Credit

Responsibility of Bank

It should be clearly understood that the Bank is not directly concerned with the proper fulfilment of the contract between the seller and the buyer. Its duty is simply to receive documents on behalf of the customer which purport to comply with the conditions stated when opening the credit.

The Bank has the right to realise the goods or to take any steps, at its discretion, with a view to safeguarding its position.

Type of Credit

Irrevocable or Revocable: It is essential that definite instructions on this point are given on all occasions. An Irrevocable Credit becomes an engagement of the Bank itself, incapable of cancellation or of modification except by consent of the beneficiary. A Revocable Credit may be cancelled without the beneficiary's consent by the customer at any time, subject, however, to the customer remaining liable in respect of any negotiation, acceptance, or payment made by the Bank through which the Credit is advised, prior to receipt of notice of cancellation by the Bank.

Availability

Expiry Date: This must always be given. The expiry date can, of course, be extended on instructions from the customer. When credits are to be opened/advised through a bank abroad, expiry dates are understood to apply to the date of negotiation, or acceptance, or payment (as the case may be) in the place abroad at which the negotiation, or acceptance, or payment is to take place, and not to the date of arrival of documents or advices in London. Credits with a London expiry date can be opened in favour of beneficiaries abroad but it is not customary to advise such credits through a foreign bank.

"Negotiated": This instruction should be used where drafts drawn by the beneficiary on Metropolitan Bank Limited either in sterling or in the currency of a country other than that of the beneficiary are to be honoured if negotiated at the place and within the period of validity of the credit.

"Accepted"/"Paid": These instructions are appropriate where the currency of the credit is that of the country of the beneficiary who is to draw drafts for acceptance on a bank abroad or claim payment from them. They are also appropriate where credits are to be opened in sterling with a London expiry date in favour of beneficiaries abroad or in favour of beneficiaries in the United Kingdom.

Documents Required

It is not sufficient to state "usual documents". The documents should be mentioned in detail. "On Board" (i.e. "shipped") Bills of Lading are normally required but if "Received for Shipment" Bills of Lading are acceptable, this should be indicated.

Short Form Bills of Lading and Bills of Lading evidencing shipment in containers will be accepted unless the credit specifically prohibits either or both of them.

† If the credit terms provide for carriage by more than one method of tranport or combined transport documents are called for without stating either the form of the documents and/or the party to issue them, the documents will be accepted as tendered, without regard to the content or to the name of the issuer.

General

Unless the credit provides otherwise, shipping documents bearing reference to extra charges in addition to the freight charges will be accepted. These charges include, for example, "Free **In/Out**" and other costs and charges incurred in container transport. Should additional charges not be acceptable the specific charges prohibited must be stated.

Unless instructions are given to the contrary, banks will take up documents presented to them up to 21 days from the date of the Bills of Lading or other shipping document, even for a short sea voyage. It is essential, therefore, for customers to calculate the maximum period they would wish to accept for presentation of documents to our correspondents abroad bearing in mind the normal airmail time required for the documents to reach us, and to stipulate the maximum number of days permitted between date of issue of the Bills of Lading or other Shipping Document and the date of presentation, even if a latest shipment date is stipulated.

FIG. 3.   *Request form for opening a documentary credit (reverse).*

the credit and not adding its confirmation, unless it has been authorised to confirm the credit.

The exporter would probably prefer a documentary credit to be a *confirmed credit,* i.e. one in which a bank in his country gives a definite undertaking either that the provisions for payment and acceptance will be duly fulfilled or, in the case of a credit available by negotiation of drafts, that the confirming bank will negotiate drafts without recourse to the drawer. It is more satisfactory to have an undertaking from a bank he knows rather than from an overseas bank about which he knows nothing. Furthermore, if he has any queries that bank is near at hand. In addition, non-payment cannot arise through exchange control restrictions in the importer's country (Article 10).

The bank establishing the credit can make the credit either *revocable* or *irrevocable.* The exporter would be wise to insist that the importer opens an irrevocable credit (*see* Fig. 4), because the terms of the credit cannot be altered without the agreement of all the parties to it. A revocable credit offers no such protection to the exporter, for it may be modified or cancelled at any time without notice to the beneficiary, but it may, of course, be considered useful by the importer who is trading with an exporter for the first time and who wishes to examine the first consignment before agreeing to an irrevocable credit. A bank has the right to be reimbursed for any payment, acceptance or negotiation made by it prior to receipt of notice of this modification or cancellation of a revocable credit (Articles 9 and 10).

An exporter will want to be satisfied that the credit has been opened for a period which will give him more than sufficient time to ship the goods, so that he will have a margin of time for any unavoidable delays. It is usual for a documentary credit to stipulate that the goods must be shipped by a certain date, and the total amount of their value. This is not always the case, however, for a *revolving credit* specifies an upper limit to the amount which can be drawn in a specified period, or an amount which can be outstanding at any one time. In addition to the latest date for shipment, credits must stipulate an expiry date for presentation of documents. When the expiry date falls on a day on which banks are closed it is extended until the first following business day (Articles 46–49).

5. Sight and acceptance credits. The difference between sight credits and acceptance credits has already been referred to in **2** above but some further comment on these two types of credit is required.

A *sight credit* usually requires the exporter to draw a sight or demand draft, and this is paid on presentation to the correspondent bank, provided that all the other terms of the credit have been complied with. Sometimes, however, no draft is required under the terms of the credit

Metropolitan Bank Limited **Overseas Branch**
PO Box XA27 606 Lothbury London EC2Z 2LM

7

Copy for advising bank

Date 3rd January

IRREVOCABLE DOCUMENTARY CREDIT	Credit number — of issuing bank: 935790	of advising bank
Advising bank	Applicant: The Downtown Import Co., Ltd., Downtown	
Beneficiary: Fabrica Speciale S/A Milan	Amount: £100,000	
	Expiry: 31st March — Date in Milan for negotiation	

Dear Sir(s)

We hereby issue in your favour this documentary credit which is available by negotiation of your draft at 90 days' sight drawn on Metropolitan Bank Ltd. Overseas Branch, PO Box XA27, 606 Lothbury London EC2Z 2LM bearing the clause: "Drawn under documentary credit No. 935790 of Metropolitan Bank Ltd." accompanied by the following documents

INVOICE
SHIPPED BILLS OF LADING in complete set to order and blank endorsed marked freight paid

INSURANCE POLICY covering marine and war risk, theft, pilferage and non-delivery, WPA for invoice amount plus 10%

CERTIFICATE OF ITALIAN ORIGIN

Covering

Shipment of 200,000 SPARKING PLUGS @ 50p each C.I.F. London

Despatch/Shipment from Genoa to London	Partial shipments Allowed	Transhipments Allowed

Special conditions

We hereby engage with drawers and/or bona fide holders that drafts drawn and negotiated in conformity with the terms of this credit will be duly honoured on presentation and that drafts accepted within the terms of this credit will be duly honoured at maturity.

The amount of each draft must be endorsed on the reverse of this credit by the negotiating bank

THE ADVISING BANK IS REQUESTED TO NOTIFY THE BENEFICIARY ADDING / WITHOUT ADDING THEIR CONFIRMATION.

Yours faithfully,
Metropolitan Bank Limited Overseas Branch
PO Box XA27 606 Lothbury London EC2Z 2LM

Countersigned

Advising bank's notification

Place, date, name and signature of the advising bank

Except so far as otherwise expressly stated, this documentary credit is subject to the "Uniform Customs and Practice for Documentary Credits" (1983 Revision), International Chamber of Commerce (Publication No. 400)

This Document conforms with the standard Form No. 1 of the I.C.C.

FIG. 4. *A documentary credit.*

and payment is made upon presentation of the documents. This is the modern tendency.

A *term* or *acceptance credit* stipulates that the beneficiary must draw a draft for a particular usance, e.g. 30, 60 or 90 days sight, or even longer. The credit may specify that the bill must be drawn upon either the correspondent bank or the issuing bank, i.e. the bank opening the credit. If it is drawn upon the issuing bank the correspondent bank (the advising bank) will usually negotiate the draft (possibly without recourse to the drawer), but if it is drawn on the correspondent bank it will signify its acceptance of the draft on the face of it and, as far as the drawer of it is concerned, he then has a credit instrument which he can either hold until maturity and then present for payment, or he can discount it. As the bill has been accepted by a bank it will be discounted at a fine rate.

6. Specimen documentary credit. Figure 4 is a specimen documentary credit which helps to illustrate the terminology so far used in this section. The specimen form has been filled in so as to relate to an imaginary shipment of sparking plugs from Genoa to London. The credit is an irrevocable credit for £100,000 providing for 90 day sight drafts to be drawn. It will be noticed that the credit stipulates that, except where otherwise expressly stated, the credit is subject to the *Uniform Customs and Practice for Documentary Credits*.

THE DOCUMENTS REQUIRED

7. The purpose of documents. Certain documents are called for in a documentary credit as evidence that the goods have been despatched and that they purport to be of the type and quality ordered. Furthermore, the documents are required to ensure that the goods are being properly transported and in order that the buyer can claim possession of the goods when they arrive.

8. The invoice. Invariably, the documentary credit will call for a commercial invoice specifying the quality and the quantity of the goods consigned and the price that is being charged. The credit may specify that the invoice must be rendered in duplicate, triplicate or in even greater numbers depending upon the needs of the importer and the requirements of his country (e.g. the customs authorities may require some copies of the invoice). The description of the goods must correspond with the description in the credit. In the remaining documents, the goods may be described in general terms (Article 41). A distinction must be drawn between a *commercial* invoice and a *pro-forma* invoice. The latter is usually sent by way of a quotation to a potential buyer, and if the terms of it are agreed the details are then transferred to the commercial invoice.

9. Transport documents. Until fairly recently the most common transport document was the marine bill of lading, but with the development of containerisation and other modern methods of transportation this is possibly not so. However, where a bill of lading is used it is of particular importance to a bank in that it is a document of title to the goods and, to some degree, has the attributes of a negotiable instrument. The goods are handed over only against surrender of the bill of lading and the holder is *prima facie* the person entitled to receive the goods. Normally bills of lading are issued in sets of three (sometimes more than three) and a fourth copy is kept by the ship's master. When one copy is handed over to claim possession of the goods, the remaining copies become void.

A bill of lading is a document signed by, or on behalf of, a master of a ship, certifying that goods have been received on board in good order for transportation and delivery as specified in the document. It does *not* amount to a contract between the exporter and the owners of the vessel to transport the goods, but does set out the terms and conditions on which the goods are transported.

The printed bill of lading, in addition to bearing the name of the vessel, has spaces for the insertion of the following details:

(a) the name of the person or firm despatching the goods;
(b) the name of the consignee;
(c) the nature of the goods;
(d) the number of packages and their identification marks;
(e) the destination of the consignment;
(f) the amount of the freight.

As it is the responsibility of the master of the ship to deliver the goods in the condition in which they are received, they are carefully inspected upon arrival on board and if they are not in good condition a note to this effect is made on the bill of lading.

A *clean* transport document, whether it be a bill of lading or the receipt of a carrier who is transporting goods by road or by some other means, is one which carries no such indication that the goods or the packaging were damaged when received on board, and it will normally stipulate that the goods were "in apparent good order and condition" when accepted. A document carrying *superimposed* comments to the effect that goods were received damaged is called a *dirty* or *foul* transport document. Banks refuse shipping documents *expressly* declaring a defective condition of the goods and/or packing, unless the credit expressly states that they may be accepted (Article 34).

Where goods are being transported by both sea and road or rail, or are to be transhipped during the voyage by sea, a *through bill of lading* or *combined transport document* may be issued covering the whole journey and these are acceptable under *Uniform Customs and Practice* provided that they do not indicate that they are subject to a charter party or that a vessel propelled by sail only is being used. *Short-form* bills of lading, i.e. simplified forms which do not contain all the details contained on a full bill of lading, may be accepted unless otherwise stated in the credit (Articles 25, 26).

Sometimes a *liner waybill* is called for in a documentary credit instead of a bill of lading and may be accepted by a bank if this is so. However, from a banker's point of view a liner waybill does not give him control over the goods for unlike a bill of lading it is not a document of title. A bank would therefore be reluctant to lend money against a set of documents which included a liner waybill. It is only evidence of a contract of carriage and a receipt by the shipping company and it does not have to be handed over to gain possession of the goods on arrival.

A transport document need state only that the goods have been taken in charge or received for shipment unless the credit calls for an on-board transport document. Where an on-board document is required this may be evidenced either by a document bearing wording indicating loading on board a named vessel, or, in the case of a transport document stating "received for shipment", by means of a notation of loading on board on the transport document signed or initialled and dated by the carrier or his agent (Article 27). Where goods are transported by sea or by more than one mode of transport, but including carriage by sea, banks do not accept a transport document stating that the goods are or will be loaded on deck, unless the credit so authorises (Article 28).

The credit may well indicate that the transport document must bear evidence that the freight charges have been paid if the terms of delivery include the cost of freight, and if this is so then banks will accept a transport document clearly indicating payment of freight by rubber stamp or some other means. The words "freight prepayable" or "freight to be prepaid" or similar words are not acceptable as constituting evidence of payment of freight. If evidence of payment of freight is not called for in the credit, then banks will accept a transport document stating that freight has yet to be paid (Article 31).

To overcome the problems that arise when goods are transported in containers banks will accept a transport document which bears a clause such as "shippers load and count" or "said by shipper to contain" (Article 32).

If goods are being despatched by post, a bank will accept as evidence of posting a post receipt or certificate if it appears to have been stamped or otherwise authenticated and dated in the place from which the credit stipulates the goods are to be despatched (Article 30).

10. The insurance policy or certificate. Where the exporter has a c.i.f. contract to supply the goods, he must insure them during transit and the importer will specify in the letter of credit that a marine and war risk insurance policy or certificate must be produced. The insurance policy must be made out in favour of the correspondent bank, or if it is made out in favour of the exporter must have his endorsement in blank when it is handed over to the bank, for, like a bill of lading, an insurance policy is freely transferable by endorsement and delivery. The Marine Insurance Act 1906 provides that the following must be specified in a marine insurance policy:

  (*a*) the name of the insurers;
  (*b*) the name of the person in whose name the insurance is effected;
  (*c*) the nature of the goods insured and the risk or risks insured against;
  (*d*) the sum or sums insured;
  (*e*) the period of insurance.

Cover notes issued by brokers may not be accepted by a bank unless specified in the credit (Article 35). The insurance document must be expressed in the same currency as the credit (Article 37), and banks must refuse insurance documents which bear a date later than the date of loading on board or despatch or taking in charge of the goods (Article 36).

11. Other documents. In addition to the invoice, transport document and insurance document, a documentary credit may require the presentation of other documents such as a *certificate of origin, certificate of quality,* or *consular invoice.*

  (*a*) *A certificate of origin* is required by some countries certifying that the goods were produced in a particular country. This would be required, for instance, where preferential rates of tariff apply to goods imported from, and definitely produced in, specific countries such as the EEC countries, between which no tariffs apply.

  (*b*) *A certificate of quality* is a certificate to the effect that the goods despatched are of the quality specified in the contract. It would have to be signed by a responsible person at the time and place of shipment. In some cases the documentary credit specifies that the goods must be tested by a particular company in the exporter's country which may take a few days. This could apply, for instance, to chemical products which need to be analysed or to metals which need to be tested for strength.

(c) *A consular invoice,* which is quite commonly required, is an invoice signed by a consul of the importing country in the country from which the goods are consigned. Often a substantial charge is made for this type of invoice and delays may be incurred in obtaining it. The exporter must bear both facts in mind in agreeing the contract of sale with the buyer and watch out that the documentary credit provides him with enough time to get the documents together.

The credit must specify by whom such other documents as these are to be issued and their wording and data content. If the credit does not do so, banks are authorised to accept the documents as presented provided that their data content makes it possible to relate the goods or services referred to in them to those referred to in the commercial invoice or to those referred to in the credit if a commercial invoice is not called for in the credit. Banks may accept any of the ancillary documents bearing a date of issuance prior to that of the credit, provided they are presented within the time limits set by the credit or in *Uniform Customs and Practice* (Articles 23 and 24).

DOCUMENTARY CREDITS AND THE BANKER

12. The contract. As far as the banker is concerned, the contract between the exporter and the importer is nothing to do with him. He must observe the terms of the documentary credit and it is the responsibility of the person opening the credit to ensure that his instructions to the bank, contained in his request to open the credit, are in accordance with the contract. It is in the banker's interest, of course, to make sure that these instructions are perfectly clear, so that there will be no dispute as to what was meant by any of them.

13. The application form. Where a credit is to be opened in the United Kingdom by an importer in favour of an exporter overseas, the importer will instruct his bank to open a credit through its correspondent in the exporter's country. The British bank will require its printed application form to be completed, which provides spaces for the essential details to be inserted and makes the task of ensuring that the instructions are clear much easier (*see* Figs. 2 and 3).

The details about the documents required are very precise. The form must also make clear whether or not partial shipments are to be permitted, and space is provided for the inclusive date up to which the credit is to be valid. On the application form it is likely that the bank will stipulate that it has the right to realise the goods, or to take any steps, at its discretion, with a view to safeguarding its position. Furthermore, the bank, in its form of indemnity which the customer must sign, is relieved of any responsibility for any error, fault or mistake and for any invalidity or irregularity in any document. These clauses might be considered very cautious practice on the part of the bank, but it must be remembered that the bank is pledging itself to carry out the terms of the credit and may find itself having to make a payment or meet a draft drawn under the credit without being able to charge it to its customer's account because the balance thereon is insufficient. For this latter reason it is quite usual to require a customer opening a credit to put up some security, or partial or total cover in the form of cash.

14. Import credits. As the name suggests, import credits are those opened by British banks in favour of exporters of goods to Britain. When the goods have been shipped to Britain, the documents called for in the credit will be received by the correspondent bank abroad and sent on to the British bank. When the documents arrive at the importer's bank they must, of course, be examined to ensure that they comply with the terms of the credit. As the correspondent bank will have checked them before paying, accepting or negotiating the draft drawn against the credit, the documents are usually in order; but discrepancies do occur and it may be necessary to contact the importer and ascertain whether or not he is prepared to overlook them. The draft drawn under the credit will accompany the documents and if it is a sight draft the overseas bank will demand reimbursement, which will be settled through the accounts of the two banks concerned. If it is a usance bill the settlement will take place when the bill matures.

15. Export credits. Where a British exporter agrees to ship his goods against a documentary credit, the importer will instruct his bank in his country to open a credit in Britain through one of the London banks. A British bank will, therefore, receive an advice from a foreign bank to the effect that the credit is to be opened. This advice may be received by letter or by cable, and not necessarily in English. The British bank involved need not be the exporter's bank and the advice passed on to the exporter may state that the documentary credit is that of the foreign bank concerned, to which the British bank does not add its confirmation, or it may be specifically stated to be a *confirmed* credit.

When the documents are produced by the exporter, the British bank must be completely satisfied that they are in order before making any payment under the credit, for if they are not in order the bank may find itself in the unenviable position of having paid the beneficiary and being unable to obtain the reimbursement from its principal, the issuing bank. A common discrepancy is for the transport document to carry a comment such as "three casks damaged" in which case the banker must safeguard himself. This he can do by asking for an indemnity from the exporter, preferably that of his bank if he is not a customer. If he is a customer of the correspondent bank, then the bank will be able to sum up its customer before overlooking any discrepancies. If considered necessary, the correspondent bank could seek the instructions of the bank opening the credit before making payment. Discrepancies in documents are the biggest problem for the banker as far as documentary credits are concerned, especially where a weak customer is involved who, for instance, is relying on a back-to-back credit or a transferable credit (*see* **17–20**).

TRANSIT CREDITS

16. Payments through London. British banks are frequently asked to arrange documentary credits in respect of trade between other countries. This is because sterling balances in London held by countries outside Britain are utilised by them to finance trade. For instance, a firm in Norway may be importing goods from Australia. This type of credit is called a *transit* or *reimbursement credit*.

BACK-TO-BACK CREDITS

17. Purchase and sale. Where a customer of a bank has had a documentary credit opened in his favour by a foreign importer of his goods, he may be able to persuade his bank to open a credit for the benefit of the original supplier of the goods, on the strength of the existing credit. The two credits are put "back-to-back", the one being issued on the security of the other. This is useful to the middleman with slender capital resources, but it would be wrong to suggest that it is only he who would want to make use of this type of credit. It is a ready means of obtaining credit for any type of firm.

18. The procedure. In opening the documentary credit on the strength of the other one, the bank concerned may require a margin to be deposited with it by the merchant, quite apart from the merchant's profit margin, which is reflected in the fact that the second credit is for a smaller sum than the first, but much would depend upon the credit-worthiness of the customer concerned. The reason for such cautiousness on the part of the bank is that there may be a short time lag between paying for the goods and receiving payment. If the trader concerned has his invoices ready in anticipation of the receipt of the documents, he may be able to arrange for both transactions to be settled on the same day. This is not always possible, however, and a time lag may well occur. The bank opening the second documentary credit (in respect of the purchase of the goods) would also have to ensure that the expiry date of the first credit (in respect of the sale) allows a margin of time for the documents to reach London, and for invoices to be changed and the documents presented to the ultimate purchaser's bank within the validity date.

Back-to-back credits are not very popular with banks and some of them will not issue them. They prefer instead to deal with the credits quite separately and not issue one on the strength of the other. There is absolutely no mention of back-to-back credits in *Uniform Customs* and hence banks are given no special protection.

TRANSFERABLE CREDITS

19. Transferring the benefit. There is a great deal of similarity between transferable credits and back-to-back credits. Both tend to be used by middlemen whose financial position is such that they have difficulty in paying for goods before they receive the proceeds from reselling them. Whereas in a back-to-back credit a second credit is opened on the strength of the first, in the case of a transferable credit the benefit of the credit opened in favour of the middleman by the purchaser is transferred to the seller of the goods.

20. The procedure. It is necessary first for the trader to insist that the credit that is opened in his favour is a transferable one. This is necessary because a documentary credit is not transferable unless it is definitely stated to be so.

Once the credit is opened by the purchaser, the trader will send an instruction to the advising bank to transfer some of the benefit of the credit to the supplier(s) of the goods. The bank will, in fact, open a credit in the supplier's favour which differs only in that it will show the trader as the buyer and a price which is less than that on the original credit. The bank should not divulge to the buyer the name of the original seller, and vice versa, nor should the original price be made known to the buyer, but the bank is protected by Article 54 of the *Uniform Customs*.

When the supplier presents his documents to the bank and receives payment, the middleman's invoices are substituted for his and forwarded with the other documents to the buyer, whose bank will reimburse the seller's bank. The middleman receives the difference in price less any expenses involved.

RED CLAUSE CREDITS

21. Packing credits. A packing or anticipatory credit, often referred to as a *red clause credit* because the credit has a clause in it printed in red, authorises the correspondent bank in the exporter's country to grant advances to the beneficiary. The issuing bank accepts responsibility for such advances, which are intended to enable the exporter to obtain his raw materials, or finance the movement of commodities such as wool, from the interior of the country to the ports. The majority of red clause credits are in respect of wool and they apply to trade with Australia and South Africa in particular. The shipper buys wool from sheep farmers inland and when he negotiates his bills drawn on the credit the correspondent bank deducts any advances made from the proceeds of the bills.

PROGRESS TEST 5

1. How can an exporter ensure that he receives payment for his goods as soon as they are shipped or very soon thereafter?   (IV, **2, 15;** V, **4–6**)

2. Distinguish between a revocable and an irrevocable documentary credit. (**4**)

3. What is meant by a confirmed credit? (**4**)

4. Enumerate the documents usually called for under a documentary credit with a brief description of their purpose. (**7–10**)

5. What is a clean transport document? (**9**)

6. What details must a banker look for on a transport document? (**9**)

7. What details does a bank require on its application form for a documentary credit? (**13**)

8. From a bank's point of view what is the difference between an import credit and an export credit? (**14, 15**)

9. What are the points of contrast and similarity between a transferable documentary credit and a back-to-back credit? (**17–20**)

10. What is a red clause credit? (**21**)

PART TWO

THE FOREIGN EXCHANGE MARKET

CHAPTER VI

Exchange Rates

FOREIGN EXCHANGE TRANSACTIONS

1. Foreign exchange. Foreign exchange is concerned with exchanging the currency of one country for that of another country. This quite obviously necessitates calculating and expressing the ratio of one currency to the other; in other words, determining a *rate of exchange*.

A system of fixed exchange rates came into existence in 1946 when the International Monetary Fund was formed, which, even though it provided for fixed parities, allowed a small variance either side of parity from day to day. The UK, for instance, which from December 1971 to June 1972 had a declared parity of $2.6057 = £1 could allow the day to day rate of exchange to fluctuate up to $2\frac{1}{4}$ per cent either side of parity. Since that date, however, there has been no agreed parity and most currencies are now allowed to float, i.e. to find their own level on the foreign exchange market. As both the fixed and floating exchange rate systems permit exchange rates to fluctuate from day to day when payments for transactions in foreign currency are to be made or received, the rate at which the two currencies change hands will be determined in the foreign exchange market. The person who needs to buy a foreign currency must pay the market price for it and, likewise, the person who has foreign currency to sell can do so at the market price. The market price (the rate of exchange) is determined by supply and demand in the same way that the market price of an ordinary commodity is determined.

2. Factors affecting supply and demand. Both the supply of, and the demand for, a currency are determined by the following factors:

(*a*) commercial transactions in goods and services;
(*b*) investment, direct and indirect, public and private;
(*c*) government loans and grants;
(*d*) transactions with international institutions;
(*e*) arbitrage;

(*f*) short-term capital movements;
(*g*) government intervention (*see* **17** below);
(*h*) confidence in the currency;
(*i*) technical factors.

3. Commercial transactions are concerned with exports and imports of both goods and services which give rise to the balance of trade and balance of payments (*see* I, **6, 7**). If imports exceed exports and the balance of trade and the balance of payments become unfavourable, foreign exchange rates will be affected in two ways. First, because imports have increased, demand for foreign currencies will have risen and, second, to buy the additional currencies more sterling will have been offered in the foreign exchange market. The extra demand for currencies will force up their values in terms of sterling and hence depreciate the value of the pound in terms of foreign currencies; the extra supply of pounds will also depreciate the value of the pound and force up the values of foreign currencies in terms of sterling.

This can be illustrated in the following way. Let us start off with the position in which the US dollar–sterling exchange rate is $1.70, and then assume that the balance of payments between Britain and the USA becomes adverse because imports of American goods have risen. Thus:

$$\$1.70 = £1 \ (\$1 = 59p)$$
$$\$1.65 = £1 \ (\$1 = 61p)$$

Because of the increased demand for US dollars, caused by the rise in imports, the value of the dollar rises in terms of sterling from 59p to, say, 61p, which means that the value of sterling in terms of dollars must move inversely from $1.70 to $1.65.

The increased supply of pounds will push the exchange rate in the same direction—the price or value of pounds will fall from $1.70 in the direction of $1.65, which means that the dollar will appreciate in value (from 59p to 61p).

4. Investments. When a company invests in plant and equipment overseas, e.g. an oil company builds a refinery, it is carrying out direct investment. Alternatively, the purchase of shares in a foreign company by a British firm, or individual, constitutes indirect investment overseas. Both are examples of private investment—investment by the private sector of the community, as distinct from government investment (public investment). Whatever the form of investment, however, the effect upon exchange rates is the same. An investment overseas necessitates the purchase of foreign currency and hence weakens the value of sterling in terms of foreign currency. An investment in Britain by non-residents, on the other hand, has the opposite effect, in that a demand for sterling is created, thus forcing up the value of sterling.

5. Government loans and grants. Loans and gifts *by* Britain to other nations tend to weaken the value of the pound because the sterling that is provided in either of these two ways may be used to buy other currencies in the foreign exchange market. This is one reason for giving "tied" loans, i.e. stipulating that the loan or grant must be used to buy British goods.

When loans are repaid, of course, they have the opposite effect upon sterling (the pound is strengthened), and interest payments also have a favourable effect upon the pound. Loans *to* Britain strengthen sterling in the foreign exchange market and weaken the value of the currency that is lent to us.

6. Transactions with international institutions. When a country subs-cribes its currency to an international institution such as the Interna-tional Monetary Fund or the International Bank for Reconstruction and Development, and that currency is used by the institution to make a loan to another member country, then it is likely to weaken the exchange rate of the country whose currency it is. If, for instance, D.marks were lent to the UK by the IMF and instead of putting the currency into our reserves we used it to settle our indebtedness, the extra D.marks would find their way on to the foreign exchange market, and, because the supply of marks will have risen, their value would fall in terms of other currencies.

7. Arbitrage. If a rate of exchange in one financial centre fell out of line with those in another centre, then by carrying out a series of swaps of currencies (arbitrage) it might be possible to make a profit. For example, if the rates of exchange are:

$$£1 = \$4$$
$$£1 = 1,000 \text{ francs}$$
$$\$1 = 250 \text{ francs}$$

and the dollar–franc rate of exchange moves to $1 = 200 francs, then it will be worth while buying 1,000 francs in London and selling them in New York. At the new rate of exchange they will yield $5, which can then be converted into pounds at $4 = £1 to produce £1.25. For every pound used by an exchange speculator in this way there is, therefore, a profit of 25p. The possibility of gain through arbitrage tends to prevent rates from fluctuating very much from parity.

8. Short-term capital movements. If interest rates are comparatively high in a financial centre, then short-term capital will be attracted to that centre and a fall in interest rates will have the opposite effect. If, for instance, the Bank of England's minimum lending rate was 10 per cent and, therefore, safe short-term investments, such as Treasury bills and local governments loans, were yielding something in the region of that rate, then it might be a profitable proposition for an American firm or institution to buy sterling with dollars and use it to invest in one of these securities. This is assuming that interest rates in New York are low and that, even after covering himself in the forward exchange market and paying a premium to do so (*see* VIII, **5**) the American financier can be sure of a bigger yield on his money in London. The demand for sterling for this purpose would tend to raise the exchange value of sterling.

9. Confidence in the currency. Capital movements to a financial centre would occur only if there was confidence in the currency concerned. If it was feared that sterling might depreciate, holders of sterling would switch their holdings into safer currencies in fear of loss through the fall in the value of the pound. British importers who have payments to make in foreign currency would obtain the currency quicker than usual (a *lead*), before the depreciation, while exporters would delay selling foreign currency proceeds until after the depreciation (a *lag*). Both leads and lags weaken the exchange rate and have an unfavourable effect upon the currency reserves.

Speculators who could foresee an appreciation in the value of a currency would buy that currency and later switch back into their own currency at the more favourable rate of exchange.

10. Technical factors. These include such factors as the reluctance to hold over the weekend balances in a currency which is in danger of depreciating, and the withdrawal of funds at particular times when returns and balance sheets have to be prepared in order to show a satisfactory position.

PURCHASING POWER PARITY (PPP)

11. The theory. The purchasing power parity theory is that *the rate of exchange between any two currencies tends to reflect their relative purchasing powers.*

According to this theory, therefore, if a sample of goods costs £1,000,000 in London or $1,700,000 in New York, the rate of exchange between the pound and the US dollar should be $1.70 = £1. This is the PPP rate.

The theory means that there is a close relationship between the internal value of a currency and its external value. If, for instance, costs and prices in the UK rose (and therefore the internal value of the pound fell) while those of the US did not rise, the cost of the sample of goods mentioned above might rise to, say, £1,100,000, giving a new PPP rate of £1.54 = £1 ($1,700,000 ÷ 1,100,000 = £1). Therefore, if the theory holds true (and there is no reason to doubt that it does *in the long run*, though not as automatically as suggested in this section) a country cannot afford to allow domestic inflation to push up its prices to a greater extent than the increase in price levels elsewhere.

12. How the theory works. If the rate of exchange between two currencies moves away from the PPP rate, changes will occur in the demand for, and supply of, currencies, which will tend to alter their values back to the PPP. This can be demonstrated by expanding on the illustration used in **3** above as follows:

$1.75 = £1 ($1 = 57p) { British goods dearer (more dollars required to buy £1's worth of goods); less demand for pounds, reduced supply of dollars. Pound becomes cheaper, dollar becomes dearer.

↓

PPP = $1.70 = £1 ($1 = 59p)

↑

$1.65 = £1 ($1 = 61p) { British goods cheaper (less dollars required to buy £1's worth of goods); more demand for pounds, increased supply of dollars. Pound becomes dearer, dollar becomes cheaper.

13. In practice. The purchasing power parity theory does tend to apply in the long run, but in the short run fluctuations in the parity are disguised by such factors as:

    (*a*) tariffs, quotas and exchange restrictions;

    (*b*) long-term and short-term capital movements;

    (*c*) confidence in the currency, which depends upon:

        (*i*) political factors; and

        (*ii*) economic factors.

It is not easy to compare the purchasing power of one currency with that of another, because living standards and ways of life vary from country to country. To decide upon a rate of exchange which reflects the two purchasing powers is, therefore, not an easy task, but time will tell whether the currency is undervalued or overvalued.

GOLD STANDARDS

14. The pre-1931 situation. Britain and most other countries of the world were on the gold standard until 1931, when the system finally broke down. Under the gold standard, a country relates the value of its currency to gold (the pound had a fixed gold content of 113.0016 grains of fine gold) and its currency is freely convertible into gold.

Because of the fixed relationships to gold, fixed parities exist between currencies and in theory an exchange rate should vary only slightly from the fixed parity (the *mint par of exchange*). This is because any movement away from the mint par of exchange would make it profitable to convert a currency into gold, ship the gold to the other financial centre, convert it into the currency of that centre and make a profit on the transactions. This ignores the cost of shipping and insuring the gold, which sets a margin either side of the mint par of exchange (the *specie points*) to which the rate of exchange can vary before there is a movement of gold.

When gold is exported, the proceeds in foreign currency are sold, reducing the value of that currency back towards the mint par of exchange. If gold is imported, then foreign currency must be bought with which to obtain the gold, and this causes the value of that currency to appreciate back towards the mint par of exchange.

15. The failure of the gold standard. It was a rule of the gold standard that a country which imported gold should increase its money supply (carry out an inflationary policy) and a country which exported gold had to decrease its money supply (pursue a deflationary policy). There was, therefore, no flexibility as far as monetary policies were concerned, for countries had to pursue the policy dictated by the flow of gold and could not adjust their monetary policies to meet their domestic needs. This inflexibility was one of the reasons for the failure of the system. Others were as follows:

(*a*) Some countries (particularly the USA and France, who were amassing gold at that time) did not use incoming gold to increase the money supply. Nor did other countries which had an outflow of gold reduce the money supply to the extent that they should have done.

(*b*) Protective trade barriers (tariffs, quotas and exchange control) were built up which impeded international trade and the growth of economies.

(*c*) Britain, for prestige reasons, returned to gold at too high a parity in 1925. She left the gold standard in 1914–25 and wanted to return to gold at the pre-war parity, which was unrealistic.

(*d*) The gold standard was blamed for the high level of unemployment. If countries could have pursued independent monetary policies, this might not have occurred.

16. The IMF system. At the Bretton Woods conference in 1944 the major nations of the world endeavoured to devise, as one of their objectives, an international monetary system which could be put into effect when the war ended, and which would have the advantages of the gold standard but not its disadvantages. As a result, the International Monetary Fund was conceived, and established in 1946.

The Fund is an institution from which countries can borrow currencies with which to finance a balance of payments deficit. Furthermore, on joining the Fund, countries had to declare a value for their currencies in terms of the US dollar, which established a system of fixed parities between the currencies of all the members. This system is demonstrated above (*see* 7), where in the example exchange rates between the dollar and the pound and the dollar and the franc established a rate of exchange for sterling and the franc. The IMF parity system worked extremely well for 25 years from 1946 onwards, despite the many revaluations and devaluations of currencies that occurred during that period. The shattering of confidence in the US dollar which resulted in its devaluation in December 1971 and in a general realignment of currencies (*the Smithsonian agreement*), and the subsequent world oil crisis and its effects upon the balance of payments of the oil-importing countries, brought an end to the IMF system of fixed parities, and if it is ever restored it will have to be a more flexible system than before.

Within the EEC the member countries (but so far not Britain) endeavour to limit fluctuations between their currencies, through the European Monetary System (*see* XIV, **16**).

17. Exchange equalisation accounts. To endeavour to ensure that their currencies do not fluctuate beyond acceptable limits, countries use the device of *exchange equalisation accounts*. Through these accounts, currencies are bought if their exchange value is low and sold if their exchange value is high, in an attempt to keep the value stable.

The UK exchange equalisation account was established in 1932, soon after the gold standard broke down. The account, which is operated by the Bank of England, was credited with the UK's reserves of foreign currencies, with which to operate on the foreign exchange market. In 1939, the Bank of England's holdings of gold (some £300 million), which up to that time had been held as partial backing for the note issue, were transferred to the account, so that it now holds all the gold and convertible currency reserves.

Taking the pre-June 1972 US dollar–sterling rate as an example, when sterling was weak and the rate fell to nearly \$2.5471 = £1, the exchange equalisation account would have been obliged to use its reserves of foreign currencies to buy up sterling in the foreign exchange market. The reduction in the supply of sterling would push up its value and the increase in the supply of other currencies cause their value, in terms of sterling, to depreciate. When sterling was strong, the account would prevent the rate from going above $2.6643 = £1 and at the same time take the opportunity of building up the reserves by selling sterling.

Exchange equalisation accounts are still used, even though the rates of exchange are floating. A government can maintain the value of its currency in terms of other currencies by using the exchange reserves or, alternatively, stop it from rising (and making its goods dearer abroad) by selling the home currency in exchange for foreign currencies.

FIXED AND FLOATING EXCHANGE RATES

18. Equilibrium rate of exchange. When the value of a country's currency, in terms of other currencies, truly reflects its purchasing power parity and the country incurs neither persistent balance of payments deficits nor surpluses, the rate of exchange between that currency and another can be said to be the equilibrium rate of exchange.

(a) *If a currency is overvalued* in terms of other currencies, then the country concerned will tend to incur balance of payments deficits. At the market rate of exchange the country's goods will be relatively dear and consequently its exports will suffer. Furthermore, as foreign goods are relatively cheap, imports will be encouraged. The balance of payments deficits, to the extent that they are financed out of the country's reserves, will cause the reserves to diminish, and if this continues for long there may be no alternative to a fall in the exchange rate.

(b) *If a currency is undervalued,* the country's goods will be relatively cheap, exports stimulated, imports discouraged, and the balance of payments favourable. Both the country's reserves and the exchange rate will rise. An increase in the value of a currency in terms of other currencies makes the country's goods dearer and tends to reduce its exports and also its balance of payments surplus.

19. The disadvantages of fixed rates. From the previous section it is obvious that the system of fixed rates of exchange requires countries to hold reserves of gold and foreign currencies with which to even out day-to-day fluctuations in exchange rates through exchange equalisation accounts, and to finance deficits in the balance of payments. When balance of payments surpluses are achieved, the reserves tend to be increased.

For countries such as Britain, whose balance of payments fortunes swing very considerably from substantial deficits to substantial surpluses, these reserves often prove insufficient. Furthermore, when a currency is as widely used as sterling, lack of confidence in it can result in very heavy drains upon the reserves in order to maintain the fixed rate of exchange.

A shortage of reserves would make a country take restrictive measures, either import controls or monetary controls, to put its balance of payments right and maintain the rate of exchange. An argument in favour of flexible exchange rates is that under such a system these measures would not be necessary. The "stop-go" monetary policies that Britain has experienced in the past could have been avoided. If there is a balance of payments deficit, then, it is claimed, the exchange rate should be allowed to depreciate freely until the country's goods become so cheap in terms of foreign currencies that exports are stimulated and the deficit is automatically rectified. A similar policy could be adopted to overcome a lack of confidence in a currency through whatever cause.

Another disadvantage of fixed rates of exchange is that it is difficult to arrive at a true purchasing power parity in the first place, so that currencies tend to be overvalued or undervalued. Such a state of affairs can build up to a point where the whole pattern of exchange rates is out of alignment and major adjustments need to be made. This was the position in 1971, when the dollar was devalued and other countries revalued to varying degrees.

20. The advantages of fixed rates. Stable exchange rates foster growth in international trade because traders can calculate fairly accurately the sum they will have to pay, or will receive, in their own currency. This is assuming that they must pay in a foreign currency for imports and receive foreign currency for exports, which would not be the case as far as British traders are concerned if settlement was to be in sterling.

If exchange rates were not fixed, traders might lose when carrying out transactions for which settlement is not to take place for some time. They could, of course, avoid loss by buying or selling currency through the forward exchange market, but nevertheless exchange fluctuations might inhibit international trade. Not only individual firms but also governments are influenced by exchange rates in deciding whether or not to import or export. A depreciation of the exchange rate would encourage a government to pursue a restrictive policy with regard to imports, while an appreciation of the rate would have the opposite effect. There is little doubt that despite the major upheavals in exchange rates that occurred from time to time they were comparatively stable under the IMF system of fixed rates, and this contributed a great deal to the remarkable growth in international trade.

Fixed exchange rates have the added advantage of avoiding the competitive depreciation of exchange rates that would tend to occur with floating exchange rates. When a currency depreciates in terms of other currencies that country's goods become cheaper to foreigners and therefore exports are stimulated. Other countries, seeing this happen, might then allow their currencies to depreciate in order to stimulate exports, with the result that in the end no country would benefit and rates of exchange would be very unstable.

PROGRESS TEST 6

1. Enumerate the factors which determine the supply of, and demand for, a currency. **(2)**

2. In what way would a rise in Britain's imports from the USA tend to cause the value of sterling to fall in terms of the US dollar? **(3)**

3. What is the connection between confidence in a currency and movements of short-term capital? **(9)**

4. What is meant by purchasing power parity? How does the theory work? **(11, 12)**

5. What factors prevent the purchasing power parity theory from applying in the short period? **(13)**

6. Why did the gold standard break down? **(15)**

7. What is the Exchange Equalisation Account, and how does it function? **(17)**

8. What is meant by (*a*) overvaluation and (*b*) undervaluation of a currency? **(18)**

9. What are the advantages and disadvantages of fixed rates of exchange? **(19, 20)**

CHAPTER VII

Terminology of the Market

THE MARKET

1. A perfect market. Students of economics will be familiar with the term "a perfect market". They will know that it means a market in which there are many buyers and sellers dealing with an homogeneous commodity, and that all are acquainted with the price being paid for the commodity throughout the market, so that there will be virtually one price for it at any particular time.

The international foreign exchange market is a near approach to a perfect market, for it deals in homogeneous "commodities" such as sterling, dollars and francs, and as buyers and sellers in the market are able to watch closely the prices of these commodities through their excellent system of communications there tends to be only one price for a currency in terms of another at any one time.

There are two types of operators in the foreign exchange market, brokers and dealers. The *brokers* are intermediaries between the banks and financial houses working on a fixed scale of commission, whereas the *dealers* (the banks and other financial houses) act as principals buying and selling on their own account, mainly, though not essentially, through the brokers.

2. The London market. In London there is no market place as such, like the Stock Exchange or Baltic Exchange, through which foreign exchange transactions are carried out. Instead the brokers and banks and other financial houses have a network of private telephone lines with one another and telecommunications with dealers overseas. The London foreign exchange market, which was closed down at the outbreak of war in 1939, when the Bank of England assumed control of the exchanges through the Exchange Control Department, was reopened in 1951. The market's affairs are managed by a committee on which there are representatives of the London Foreign Exchange Bankers' Committee and the London Foreign Exchange Brokers' Association.

Since 1951, freedom has gradually been restored to the market and dealers and brokers are now allowed to work without restriction.

Arbitrage is permitted and it is permissible to "run a position". In "running a position" a dealer deliberately ends the working day with more of a currency than was required for the day's transactions, in the hope that the value of the currency will appreciate and a profit will be made. Alternatively, if it is thought that the value of a currency will fall (i.e. become cheaper in terms of the home currency) more of a currency will be sold than has been purchased, in the hope that the additional units required can be purchased later at the more favourable rate.

The London banks have accounts in foreign currencies with a large number of banks in foreign centres. These accounts are drawn upon by selling credit instruments such as drafts and mail transfers to their customers and by the banks' sales of currencies in the foreign exchange market. Conversely they are credited with credit instruments drawn in foreign currency and payable to London banks and with purchases of the foreign currency concerned by the London banks in the exchange market. The various departments of the London banks must, therefore, keep a close account of their transactions with the foreign banks so that the overall position can be readily ascertained.

As we saw in II, the accounts a bank keeps with other banks are called *nostro* ("our") accounts by that bank, and the accounts which it keeps for other banks are called *vostro* ("your") accounts.

RATES OF EXCHANGE

3. Method of quotation. Rates of exchange in the UK are now expressed as so many units of a foreign currency per unit of the home currency, e.g. $1.6657 = £1. The foreign exchange market always quotes two rates of exchange (e.g. $1.6657–62). One rate is the dealer's buying rate and the other is his selling rate.

The foreign exchange dealer will employ the maxim "*buy high, sell low*". In other words, he will want to get as many units of foreign currency as he can for each pound he pays, and he will give as few units of foreign currency as possible for every pound paid to him. For instance, if the quotation is $1.6657–62 he will buy dollars at 1.6662 and sell dollars at 1.6657. The difference between his buying and his selling price is his profit margin.

4. Favourable and unfavourable rates. From an individual's point of view, a high rate of exchange is favourable to the person who owes foreign currency because he receives more units of the foreign currency for each unit of the home currency than he would if the rate were lower.

To the person who is owed foreign currency, a high rate is an unfavourable rate because, in selling the currency which he receives, he must hand over more units per unit of the home currency than he would have to if the rate were lower.

From a national point of view, a high rate is favourable as the currency is worth more in terms of foreign currency, but this is not so if a currency is overvalued as it then becomes too difficult for a country to sell its goods abroad.

Several other terms are used in the foreign exchange market to denote favourable and unfavourable movements in exchange rates, and to understand these more readily the following examples should be studied.

$1.77 = £1	Rate has *risen*. More *favourable* from national point of view. More *favourable* to individual who owes dollars. Dollar is *weaker* or *easier*. Dollars are *cheaper*. Pound has *appreciated* in terms of dollars.
↑ ↓	
$1.66 = £1	Rate has *fallen*. *Unfavourable* from national point of view. *Unfavourable* to individual who owes dollars. Dollar is *firmer* or *harder*. Dollars are *dearer*. Pound has *depreciated* in terms of dollars.

5. Cross-rates of exchange. As has been shown (*see* VI, **7**), through arbitrage transactions it is possible to make a profit by taking advantage of temporary variations in the rate of exchange. Exchange dealers carefully watch for opportunities to make profits in this way, and therefore there is little movement away from the cross-rate of exchange. Cross-rates are calculated by comparing the quotations for any two currencies in terms of a third. Reverting to the example used in VI, **7**:

$$\$? = £1$$
$$\text{if } £1 = 1,000 \text{ francs}$$
$$\text{and } \$1 = 250 \text{ francs.}$$

From this it is obvious that the cross-rate of exchange for the dollar and the pound must be $4 = £1.

6. The spot rate. The normal rate of exchange quoted in the market is the *spot* rate. This is the "basic" rate or TT rate of exchange, that is, the rate for transactions in which the funds are to be paid over in each centre virtually on the same day so that no loss of interest is involved. In actual fact such transactions (apart from those between bank and customer which are carried out the same day) are completed two days after the agreement to buy and sell. Spot rate is also the basic rate in that it is the rate from which rates for particular types of remittances and forward rates are calculated.

7. Premium and discount. These terms relate to the value of a currency in the forward exchange market. If a currency is at a *premium* then it is *dearer*; i.e. fewer units of it can be obtained for every pound than at the spot rate. When a currency is at a *discount* it is *cheaper*, i.e. more units can be obtained for each pound than at the spot rate (these terms are more fully discussed in VIII).

FOREIGN EXCHANGE TABLES AND ARTICLES

8. Specimen tables. Tables IV and V, reproduced from the *Financial Times* of 17th July 1984, illustrate how exchange rates are quoted in London. It will be seen that the rates for the US and Canadian dollars take precedence, the rates for other countries' currencies following in alphabetical order of financial centres. Other newspapers publish all the rates in alphabetical order of countries.

There are two sets of spot rates, the *day's spread* and the *close*. The figures under the day's spread show the highest and lowest rates that were quoted during the previous day, whereas the rates in the "close" column are those which ruled at the close of business on that day. As is to be expected, the day's spread is much wider than the margins in the rates at the close of day.

By consulting Table VI showing exchange cross-rates, it is possible to ascertain the quotations by one financial centre on another for the ten principal centres. Table V, showing forward rates, will be discussed more fully in Chapter VIII.

9. Commonwealth rates of exchange. Under the heading "other currencies" in Table IV, several rates for Commonwealth countries are quoted. These are quoted in terms of units of the Commonwealth country's currency per £1, e.g. 1.5810–1.5840 Australian Dollars = £1.

10. Rates to the customer. The rates of exchange quoted in the London press relate to the prices at which foreign exchange dealers carried out transactions with one another on the previous day. The banks buy from, and sell currencies to, their customers at rates of exchange notified to branches each day that are closely related to the market rates on the previous day.

11. World value of the pound. The table in Appendix I, listing the value of the pound in terms of local currencies throughout the world, is given for easy reference. It has been taken from the *Financial Times* for 17th July 1984.

12. Daily press comments. Students can help to familiarise themselves with the terminology of the foreign exchange market by reading the daily comment in the financial press on the developments in the foreign exchange market on the previous day.

The following extracts from articles in the financial press are followed by translations into phraseology which can be more readily understood.

(*a*) ***Sterling improved slightly against the US dollar, rising 10 points to $1.6535. A moderate business was done, and the pound's gain was registered in spite of a general demand for dollars from the Continent.***

TABLE IV. SPOT RATES OF EXCHANGE

	Day's spread	*Close*
US	1.3160–1.3290	1.3255–1.3265
Canada	1.7505–1.7630	1.7580–1.7590
Netherlands	4.1965–4.2305	4.21½–4.22½
Belgium	75.47–76.02	75.65–76.80
Denmark	13.62¾–13.70	13.66½–13.67½
Ireland	1.2155–1.2230	1.2200–1.2210
West Germany	3.7195–3.75	3.73½–3.74½
Portugal	195.2–203	196¼–203
Spain	211.2–212.5	212.3–212.5
Italy	2,287–2,309	2,299–2,301
Norway	10.75¼–10.84¼	10.82–10.83
France	11.41½–11.50½	11.48½–11.49½
Sweden	10.90½–10.99	10.94½–10.95½
Japan	317.3–319.5	318¼–319¼
Austria	26.15–26.30	26.25–26.30
Switzerland	3.14¼–3.17	3.15½–3.16½

Belgian rate is for convertible francs. Financial franc 76.65–76.75.

OTHER CURRENCIES

	£	$
Argentina Peso	73.01–73.06	55.19–55.25
Australia Dollar	1.5810–1.5840	1.1950–1.1960
Brazil Cruzeiro	2,381.40–2,395.12	1,800–1,809
Finland Markka	7.9288–7.9481	5.9750–5.9800
Greek Drachma	147.184–147.935	111.40–111.90
Hong Kong Dollar	10.367–10.377	7.8185–7.8235
Iran Rial	118.50*	90.25*
Kuwait Dinar (KD)	0.39505–0.39575	0.29875–0.29900
Luxembourg Franc	75.65–75.80	57.12–57.12
Malaysia Dollar	3.1010–3.1070	2.3385–2.3400
Saudi Arabian Riyal	4.6425–4.6470	3.5105–3.5100
Singapore Dollar	2.8350–2.8410	2.1380–2.1395
South African Rand	1.9449–1.9507	1.4675–1.4700
UAE Dirham	4.85600–4.85615	3.6720–3.6730

* Selling rate.

NOTE RATES

	£
Austria	26.05–26.35
Belgium	76.00–76.80
Denmark	13.60–13.74
France	11.41–11.52
Germany	3.71¼–3.75¼
Italy	2,280–2,310
Japan	318–322
Netherlands	4.19–4.23
Norway	10.75–10.86
Portugal	191–198
Spain	205–214
Sweden	10.88–10.99
Switzerland	3.14–3.17
United States	1.31½–1.33½
Yugoslavia	188–196

TABLE V. FORWARD RATES

	One month	*% pa*	*Three months*	*% pa*
US	0.08–0.04 c pm	0.54	0.02–0.08 dis	–0.15
Canada	0.01–0.11c dis	–0.41	0.41–0.52 dis	–1.06
Netherlands	$2\frac{3}{8}$–2c pm	6.22	$5\frac{7}{8}$–$5\frac{3}{8}$ pm	5.33
Belgium	8–3c pm	0.86	12–4 pm	0.42
Denmark	$\frac{3}{8}$øre pm–$\frac{1}{8}$ dis	0.22	$1\frac{1}{8}$–$\frac{1}{4}$ pm	0.20
Ireland	0.03p pm–0.08 dis	–0.25	0.17–0.34 dis	–0.84
West Germany	$2\frac{1}{4}$–2pf pm	6.82	$5\frac{5}{8}$–$5\frac{3}{8}$ pm	5.88
Portugal	20–160c dis	–5.41	100–510 dis	–6.11
Spain	20–50c dis	–1.98	105–145 dis	–2.35
Italy	6–8lire dis	–3.65	21–25 dis	–4.00
Norway	$\frac{1}{8}$–$\frac{7}{8}$øre dis	–0.55	$1\frac{1}{2}$–$2\frac{1}{4}$ dis	–0.69
France	1–$\frac{1}{8}$c pm	0.59	par–$1\frac{1}{4}$ dis	–0.22
Sweden	1–$1\frac{1}{8}$öre dis	–1.16	$3\frac{1}{8}$–$3\frac{3}{4}$ dis	–1.26
Japan	$1\frac{7}{8}$–$1\frac{5}{8}$y pm	6.59	$4\frac{1}{2}$–$4\frac{1}{8}$ pm	5.41
Austria	$13\frac{1}{2}$–$11\frac{7}{8}$gro pm	5.79	$35\frac{3}{8}$–$31\frac{3}{8}$ pm	5.08
Switzerland	$2\frac{1}{4}$–$1\frac{7}{8}$c pm	7.83	$5\frac{3}{4}$–$5\frac{1}{8}$ pm	6.88

The rate for sterling in terms of the US dollar rose by 10 points from $1.6525 to $1.6535. This was an improvement in the rate as far as sterling is concerned, as Britain now gets more dollars for every pound. There were a moderate number of dealings in sterling and dollars. The improvement in the rate was rather unexpected in view of the fact that there was a general demand for dollars in the financial centres of the Continent, which tended to improve the value of the dollar in terms of other currencies. (The improvement in the sterling–dollar rate must, of course, mean that the value of the dollar fell in terms of sterling.)

(*b*) *On the spot, sterling weakened slightly in terms of the D.mark by $\frac{1}{2}$ to 4.03; but made good progress against the Belgian franc and the guilder.*

In terms of the D.mark, sterling became worth less in the spot market, the rate falling from $4.03\frac{1}{2}$ to 4.03. In terms of the Belgian franc and the Dutch guilder, sterling became worth more, the rates for these two currencies having risen.

(*c*) *The rise in the French Bank Rate made little difference to the rate for the franc.*

A rise in the French Bank Rate would tend to attract short-term funds to France for investment. Foreigners would buy francs with their own currencies with the intention of investing the francs at the more

TABLE VI. EXCHANGE CROSS-RATES

	Pound sterling	US dollar	Deutsche mark	Japanese yen	French franc
Pound sterling	1.	1.326	3.740	318.8	11.49
US dollar	0.754	1.	2.821	240.4	8.665
Deutsche mark	0.267	0.355	1.	85.23	3.072
Japanese yen (1,000)	3.137	4.160	11.73	1000.	36.05
French franc (10)	0.870	1.154	3.255	277.4	10
Swiss franc	0.316	0.420	1.184	100.9	3.636
Dutch guilder	0.237	0.314	0.886	75.53	2.723
Italian lira (1,000)	0.435	0.577	1.626	138.6	4.996
Canadian dollar	0.569	0.754	2.127	181.3	6.534
Belgian franc (100)	1.321	1.751	4.939	420.9	15.17

	Swiss franc	Dutch guilder	Italian lira	Canadian dollar	Belgian franc
Pound sterling	3.160	4.220	2,300	1.759	75.73
US dollar	2.383	3.183	1,735	1.326	57.11
Deutsche mark	0.845	1.128	615.0	0.470	20.25
Japanese yen (1,000)	9.914	13.24	7216.	5.517	237.6
French franc (10)	2.750	3.673	2,002	1.530	65.91
Swiss franc	1.	1.335	727.8	0.556	23.96
Dutch guilder	0.749	1.	545.0	0.417	17.94
Italian lira (1,000)	1.374	1.835	1,000	0.765	32.92
Candian dollar	1.797	2.400	1,308	1.	43.06
Belgian franc (100)	4.173	5.573	3,037	2.322	100

favourable rates of interest in France. This made little difference to the sterling–franc exchange rate, however.

(d) *The decline in hopes of a fall in interest rates following the news of a wider trade gap in January again weakened the forward pound, the three-month discount rising 6 points to 1.87 cents.*

Because an early fall in interest rates seems remote in view of the widening of the gap between imports and exports in January, the supply of forward pounds rose and they became cheaper, the three-month discount rising 6 points to 1.87 cents. This weakening in forward sterling was caused by the fact that US investors were encouraged to invest their funds in the UK by the continuation of the high level of interest rates, demanding forward dollars (in exchange for sterling) to cover the repatriation of their dollars in the future at a rate to be fixed now. The supply of forward sterling thus rose, making its value lower (an increase in the discount); therefore the dollar premium increased.

(e) *The renewed uncertainty over the outlook for the pound was reflected in the rate for Euro-sterling. Deposits at short-term were attracting 8 per cent whereas a week ago the rate was $7\frac{1}{8}$ per cent.*

The renewed uncertainty over the outlook for the pound caused the rate of interest paid on sterling deposits to rise. Deposits at short-term notice were attracting 8 per cent, whereas a week ago the rate was $7\frac{1}{8}$ per cent. The rise occurred because it is likely that interest rates in London will remain high, and those persons or institutions wanting to borrow sterling will still find Euro-sterling a little cheaper than borrowing sterling in London.

(f) *Sterling rose just over 7 points against the US dollar to 1.8724, its highest since early June. The Bank of England appeared to make further, if limited, purchases of dollars for the reserves.*

Sterling rose 7 points against the US dollar to $1.8724, its highest since early June. This favourable movement in the rate enabled the Bank of England to make further, if limited, purchases of dollars for the reserves through the Exchange Equalisation Account. Under the circumstances, the Bank could sell sterling for dollars to a modest extent without causing the exchange value of sterling to fall (though it might have risen still further if the action had not been taken).

(g) *In forward dealings, however, the tone of the pound was softer.*

In the forward market the pound became cheaper, the discount having increased slightly (or, alternatively, the dollar premium was reduced).

(h) *The premiums on dollars in the forward market all widened significantly, the premium on three-month dollars jumping 6 points to 1.57 cents.*

The dollar became dearer in the forward market, the premiums for forward transactions for all lengths of time having increased, the premium on three-month dollars jumping from 1.51 cents to 1.57 cents.

PROGRESS TEST 7

1. What is meant by "running a position" in the foreign exchange market? (**2**)

2. How are rates of exchange quoted? What maxim does an exchange dealer employ in deciding which is the buying rate and which is the selling rate? (**3–7**)

3. What is meant by a favourable rate of exchange (a) to a nation (b) to a person who is owed some of the foreign currency concerned? (**4**)

4. When the dollar–sterling rate (e.g. $1.67 = £1) of exchange has risen:

(a) Is the rate more favourable or less favourable from the point of view of the UK?

(*b*) Is the dollar weaker or firmer?

(*c*) Are dollars cheaper or dearer?

(*d*) Has the pound appreciated or depreciated in terms of the dollar?   **(4)**

5. In foreign exchange tables what is the difference between the *day's spread* and the *close*?   **(8)**

CHAPTER VIII

Forward Exchange

ELIMINATION OF EXCHANGE RISKS

1. Fixing the price of goods. When an exporter quotes the price of his goods in a foreign currency he wants to be sure of receiving sufficient in his own currency to cover his costs of production and a reasonable profit. If, in the meantime, the value of his own currency appreciates in terms of the other currency, he stands to make a loss on the transaction. This can be avoided by selling the foreign currency in advance through the forward exchange market.

Similarly, the importer who has to pay for his goods in foreign currency will want to know how much the goods are going to cost him in terms of his own currency. He, too, can make certain by using the forward exchange market. He can buy the currency in advance through that market.

The essence of a forward exchange contract with a bank is to fix at once a price for the purchase or sale of a prescribed amount of foreign currency at some future date. The bank commits itself to selling or buying the currency at an agreed rate of exchange and can cover itself by matching a contract to sell with a contract to buy, and vice versa. In this way, both the bank and its customer are freed from the risk of loss through fluctuations in the exchange rate. If, in the interval between signing the forward exchange contract and the date of its completion, the person who buys currency finds that the price of the foreign currency has risen in terms of his own currency, then he has saved himself a loss; but on the other hand, if the exchange rate moves in his favour, then he would have gained if he had waited until the day on which he wanted the currency and bought it on the spot market. But he cannot have it both ways.

2. Other transactions. Forward exchange contracts are also invaluable to persons other than importers and exporters of goods. Any debtor who has a payment in foreign currency to make at a future date can fix the rate of exchange through the forward market. A creditor who is to receive a payment in foreign currency can sell at once for delivery at some future date.

Speculators out to invest their funds in the financial centre which offers the highest level of interest rates also find the forward exchange market useful. An American, for instance, who has bought sterling with dollars and invested the sterling in UK Treasury bills of 91 days' tenor, can ensure that he does not make a loss on repatriating his funds when the bills mature. He can do this by buying dollars three months ahead in the forward exchange market. The forward dollars may be a little dearer or a little cheaper than spot dollars, depending upon supply and demand.

3. Fixed rates of exchange. Even when the value of sterling was fixed in terms of the US dollar through the International Monetary Fund, an importer or exporter stood to make a loss through fluctuations in the exchange rate and thus forward exchange contracts were necessary. For instance, when we last had a fixed parity (of $2.6057 = £1) this could fluctuate by up to $2\frac{1}{4}$ per cent either side of the parity rate, i.e. up to $2.6643 and down to $2.5471 = £1. An importer, therefore, who had to find $266,430 in (say) three months' time and reckoned that they would cost him £100,000 because the current spot rate was $2.6643, might have had the misfortune of having to pay £104,600 when the time came to buy the dollars, if the rate had deteriorated to $2.5471. It would therefore be worth while paying a premium of a fraction of a cent per dollar, or even a cent or more, to buy the dollars forward if there was a likelihood of sterling depreciating in this way.

Since sterling has been allowed to float, from June 1972, forward cover has become even more advisable, of course.

4. The contract. When a bank agrees to buy or sell forward exchange it requires its customer to sign a contract, but between themselves exchange dealers carry on business, as in the spot market, by verbal agreement, followed later by written confirmation.

As far as the banker–customer relationship is concerned, a written agreement is necessary, as the bank stands to make a loss if the customer fails to fulfil his pledge to either buy or sell currency. A bank which has bought some foreign currency from a customer for delivery at some future date will have covered itself by selling that currency forward. If its customer is unable to produce the currency on the due date, then the bank will have to buy some spot in order to meet its commitment to sell and this may have to be done at a rate less favourable to the bank than that which was agreed upon with the customer.

FORWARD EXCHANGE QUOTATIONS

5. Premiums and discounts. Forward exchange rates are quoted in terms of premiums and discounts on the spot rates. This can be seen from Table V, which gives the forward quotations for sixteen major currencies. Where the forward rate is at a premium the abbreviation *pm* is used. A discount is shown as *dis* and the word *par* means that the forward rate is at a parity with the spot rate.

A premium is under spot, i.e. the rate is lower than the spot rate, and a discount is over spot, i.e. the rate is higher than spot rate. This is because a premium means that a currency is dearer and therefore fewer units of it will be received for each pound and a discount means that a currency is cheaper.

6. Examples of forward rates. The following two examples illustrate the reasoning involved in calculating forward rates. Taking first of all the Italian lira as an example of a currency at a premium, the spot rate at the close of business might be quoted at 2,402–03 and the premiums as $5\frac{1}{2}$–$4\frac{1}{2}$ lire and 12–11 lire for one month and three months respectively. On the basis of the maxim "buy high, sell low", it can be seen that the dealer will buy spot at 2,403 and sell at 2,402. The premiums must be *deducted* from the spot because a premium means that the lira is dearer. Because the dealer will want as many lire as possible for every pound, he will deduct the lower premium figure to obtain his buying price and the higher figure for his selling price. The rates will therefore be calculated as follows:

	Dealer's selling price	Dealer's buying price
Spot	2,402	2,403
Premium	$5\frac{1}{2}$	$4\frac{1}{2}$
One month's forward rate	$2,396\frac{1}{2}$	$2,398\frac{1}{2}$

	Dealer's selling price	Dealer's buying price
Spot	2,402	2,403
Premium	12	11
Three months' forward rate	2,390	2,392

An example of a currency often quoted at a discount is the Swedish krona. Let us take the spot rate as being 9.97–98, the forward discount for one month as par—1 öre—and the discount for three months as $\frac{1}{2}$–$1\frac{1}{2}$ öre. Again we must use the maxim "buy high, sell low". The dealer will therefore buy spot at 9.98 and sell at 9.97. The discount must be *added* because discount means cheaper. As the dealer will want as many kronor as possible for each pound, the larger discount figure will be added to his buying price and the lower figure to his selling price. The forward rates will therefore work out as follows:

	Dealer's selling price	Dealer's buying price
Spot discount	9.97	9.98
	Nil	1
One month's forward rate	9.97	9.99

	Dealer's selling price	Dealer's buying price
Spot	9.97	9.98
Discount	$\frac{1}{2}$	$1\frac{1}{2}$
Three months' forward rate	$9.97\frac{1}{2}$	$9.99\frac{1}{2}$

The quotations given in the press are for one month and three months. It is, however, possible to obtain a quotation for six months and also for an odd period such as 57 days. Quotations for broken periods are not usually in strict proportion and tend to be less favourable.

7. Option forwards. If a person knows approximately when he will need some foreign currency or when he will have some for disposal, but is not able to give an exact date, he can enter into an option forward contract as distinct from an ordinary fixed forward contract. It is essential to note that *this is not an option to deal*. The deal must be completed, but there is *option as to the date of completion of the contract*.

The bank customer who knows for certain that he will require some of a currency or will have some of a currency to sell between two dates can enter into a contract for completion some time during that period, at his option.

In calculating the rate at which he will enter into such a contract a dealer will assume that the customer will want to complete the contract at the worst possible time from the dealer's point of view. He will, therefore, use whichever rate (at the beginning or end or, conceivably, the middle of the option period) is least favourable to the customer. Table VII illustrates how the rates are compiled. For the sake of continuity the forward quotations for lire and kronor in the previous example have been used. Imaginary rates for two months' fixed forwards have been inserted.

The basis on which the forward option rates are calculated is shown in Tables VIII and IX. It is essential to remember that the dealer will always buy high and sell low.

TABLE VII. OPTION FORWARD RATES

Italian lire (premium)	Dealer's selling price	Dealer's buying price
Spot	2,402	2,403
1 month forward fixed	2,396$\frac{1}{2}$	2,398$\frac{1}{2}$
1 month forward option	2,396$\frac{1}{2}$	2,403
2 months forward fixed	2,393$\frac{1}{2}$	2,395$\frac{1}{2}$
2 months forward, option over 2 months	2,393$\frac{1}{2}$	2,403
2 months forward, option over 2nd month	2,393$\frac{1}{2}$	2,398$\frac{1}{2}$
3 months forward fixed	2,390	2,392
3 months forward, option over 3 months	2,390	2,403
3 months forward, option over 2nd and 3rd months	2,390	2,398$\frac{1}{2}$
3 months forward, option over 3rd month	2,390	2,395$\frac{1}{2}$

Swedish kronor (discount)	Dealer's selling price	Dealer's buying price
Spot	9.97	9.98
1 month forward fixed	9.97	9.99
1 month forward option	9.97	9.99
2 months forward fixed	9.97$\frac{1}{4}$	9.99$\frac{1}{4}$
2 months forward, option over 2 months	9.97	9.99$\frac{1}{4}$
2 months forward, option over 2nd month	9.97	9.99$\frac{1}{4}$
3 months forward fixed	9.97$\frac{1}{2}$	9.99$\frac{1}{2}$
3 months forward, option over 3 months	9.97	9.99$\frac{1}{2}$
3 months forward, option over 2nd and 3rd months	9.97	9.99$\frac{1}{2}$
3 months forward, option over 3rd month	9.97$\frac{1}{4}$	9.99$\frac{1}{2}$

8. Close-outs and extensions. Where a customer has entered into a contract to sell foreign currency to a bank and, because the payment he was expecting has not arrived, he is unable to fulfil his contract, the bank will sell him the currency he needs at the spot rate on the day of completion so that he can then sell it back to the bank at the rate agreed in the forward contract. This is called a close-out. In reality the bank will simply debit or credit the customer with the difference between the spot rate and the forward rate as well as credit the customer with the

TABLE VIII. OPTION FORWARD RATES: BASIS OF CALCULATION. ITALIAN LIRE (PREMIUM)

	Rate at beginning of option period		Rate at end of option period		Rate less favourable to customer
Selling rates					
1 month forward option	Spot	2,402	1 month forward	2,396½	2,396½
2 months forward, option over 2 months	Spot	2,402	2 months forward	2,393½	2,393½
2 months forward, option over 2nd month	1 month forward	2,396½	2 months forward	2,393½	2,393½
3 months forward, option over 3 months	Spot	2,402	3 months forward	2,390	2,390
3 months forward, option over 2nd and 3rd months	1 month forward	2,396½	3 months forward	2,390	2,390
3 months forward, option over 3rd month	2 months forward	2,393½	3 months forward	2,390	2,390
Buying rates					
1 month forward option	Spot	2,403	1 month forward	2,398½	2,403
2 months forward, option over 2 months	Spot	2,403	2 months forward	2,395½	2,403
2 months forward, option over 2nd month	1 month forward	2,398½	2 months forward	2,395½	2,398½
3 months forward, option over 3 months	Spot	2,403	3 months forward	2,392	2,403
3 months forward, option over 2nd and 3rd months	1 month forward	2,398½	3 months forward	2,392	2,395½
3 months forward, option over 3rd month	2 months forward	2,395½	3 months forward	2,392	2,395½

TABLE IX. OPTION FORWARD RATES: BASIS OF CALCULATION.
SWEDISH KRONOR (DISCOUNT)

	Rate at beginning of option period		Rate at end of option period	Rate less favourable to customer
Selling rates				
1 month forward option	Spot	9.97	1 month forward	9.97	9.97
2 months forward, option over 2 months	Spot	9.97	2 months forward	9.97¼	9.97
2 months forward, option over 2nd month	1 month forward	9.97	2 months forward	9.97¼	9.97
3 months forward, option over 3 months	Spot	9.97	3 months forward	9.97½	9.97
3 months forward, option over 2nd and 3rd months	1 month forward	9.97	3 months forward	9.97½	9.97
3 months forward, option over 3rd month	2 months forward	9.97¼	3 months forward	9.97½	9.97¼
Buying rates				
1 month forward option	Spot	9.98	1 month forward	9.99	9.99
2 months forward, option over 2 months	Spot	9.98	2 months forward	9.99¼	9.99¼
2 months forward, option over 2nd month	1 month forward	9.99	2 months forward	9.99¼	9.99¼
3 months forward, option over 3 months	Spot	9.98	3 months forward	9.99½	9.99½
3 months forward, option over 2nd and 3rd months	1 month forward	9.99	3 months forward	9.99½	9.99½
3 months forward, option over 3rd month	2 months forward	9.99¼	3 months forward	9.99½	9.99½

proceeds under the forward contract. A close-out could also occur if an importer who had entered into a forward contract to buy foreign currency found that he did not require it, or some of it, after all, and the same principles would be applied. Where a contract has been closed-out it may be extended forward to a new date. This is usually done by entering into a new forward exchange contract with an adjustment for the close-out.

An example of a close-out and an extension is given in X, Specimen Question 3, which deals with exchange arithmetic, and the reader should refer to that example in order to more fully understand the principles involved. When a bank extends a contract it will usually be generous to its customer and deduct the forward *buying* premium from the spot *selling* rate or the forward *selling* premium from the spot *buying* rate when determining the rate for the extended contract, depending upon whether the bank is buying or selling. In X, Specimen Question 3, the bank is therefore willing to quote a rate of 13.31 instead of $13.35\frac{1}{2}$ to its customer for the extension, i.e. it will give the customer more francs for every pound than it would do under a normal contract. This is called the *diagonal rule* and is employed only by the British banks. On the date of the close-out (1st March) the bank's buying rate is 13.36 and this is the rate at which it buys francs from the customer in order that he may complete his second forward contract (the close-out). On the same day the bank would normally offer a one-month forward option contract to sell francs at $13.35\frac{1}{2}$ less 5 cents premium = $13.30\frac{1}{2}$, but in extending the contract it will use its spot buying rate instead (13.36) and take the 5 cents premium from that to arrive at 13.31 as its forward selling rate.

FACTORS AFFECTING FORWARD RATES

9. Confidence in a currency. If they have sufficient confidence in a currency, investors who have purchased that currency in order to invest it will leave themselves uncovered, i.e. they will not sell the currency forward in exchange for their own. The "confidence" here referred to is confidence that the currency will not depreciate. Obviously, if it is feared that a currency will depreciate, holders of it will either switch into another currency as soon as possible or sell it forward. Consequently, both the spot rate and the forward rate for the currency will depreciate because of the fear that its value will fall. Hence a lack of confidence in a currency tends to feed upon itself. For the forward rate this would probably mean a discount in terms of other currencies, which means that the other currencies would be at a premium in terms of that currency.

Where funds are being attracted to a country by high interest rates and the investors concerned are covering the repatriation of their funds through the forward exchange market, the spot rate will appreciate while the forward rate will depreciate. For example, if Americans were selling dollars for pounds in order to invest the pounds in British Treasury bills, the extra demand for pounds would cause the spot rate to appreciate, while the extra supply of sterling in the forward market in exchange for dollars might cause sterling to go to a discount and the dollar to go to a premium. The premium on the forward dollar is an expense to the American which he must set against the higher interest yield he is receiving by investing in a centre where interest rates are high. The competition among investors will tend to make the gap between the interest differential and the forward premium a narrow one, and the level of interest rates in the two countries concerned is obviously a very important factor in the determination of the forward rate of exchange.

Movements of short-term capital (often referred to as *hot money*) can cause the forward margins to follow an abnormal pattern. In fact, at such times it is very difficult to assess all the factors on which the forward rates are based.

Confidence affects traders as well as investors. A lack of confidence in a currency will cause the leads and lags referred to in VI, 9. As with spot rates, forward rates depend a great deal upon the foresight and upon the whims and fancies of foreign exchange dealers. Their transactions in the forward market reflect their views on future movements in exchange rates. Forward rates are also dependent upon technical factors, such as the approach of weekends and return days.

The factors determining forward rates are therefore very similar to those which determine spot rates but, in addition, forward rates depend upon the spot rates themselves.

10. Government intervention. Since 1964 the British government has used the exchange equalisation account to intervene in the forward exchange market. By doing this it is possible to delay a drain upon the exchange reserves and a lead on imports. By buying sterling in the forward market the government reduces the forward discount and will thus encourage importers who are wanting to purchase foreign currency in advance of requirements to do so in the forward market rather than the spot market. (If the discount was very high the importer might prefer to buy spot currency and convert it abroad until it was required.) The smaller discount would also encourage foreign exporters to sell sterling proceeds forward rather than borrow sterling and sell it spot to avoid loss through depreciation of sterling. The intervention thus relieves the spot rate when it is most in need of support, by deferring sales of sterling.

PROGRESS TEST 8

1. What is the purpose of entering into a forward exchange contract with a bank? **(1–3)**

2. When a currency is at a premium is it cheaper or dearer? Does one receive more of it or less of it per unit of the home currency? **(VII, 7; VIII, 5)**

3. Having ascertained the spot quotation for a currency (e.g. DM $8.30\frac{3}{4}$–$31\frac{1}{2}$) and the one month forward premium (e.g. $3\frac{7}{8}$–$3\frac{3}{8}$ pf. pm), how is the rate at which a dealer will (a) sell, (b) buy, one month forward calculated? **(6)**

4. What precisely is an option forward contract? Has the bank customer an option to deal? **(7)**

5. On what basis are exchange rates for option forwards calculated? What is meant by taking the less favourable of two rates from the customer's point of view? **(7)**

6. What is meant by a close-out of a forward exchange contract? **(8)**

7. What factors determine the forward margins on a currency? **(9, 10)**

8. Define the term "hot money". **(9)**

9. Why does the UK government intervene in the forward exchange market? **(10)**

CHAPTER IX

The Euro-currency Market

FOREIGN CURRENCY DEPOSITS

1. Receipt and use of deposits. The term *Euro-currency* is one which arose about 30 years ago to describe deposits of currency which are owned by non-residents of the country whose currency it is, and which are lent by their owners. For instance, a bank in France whose account with a London bank was credited with sterling from an external source would be in the possession of Euro-sterling. The French bank would be able to put this sterling to good use by lending it at comparatively high rates of interest to those anxious to borrow sterling. Euro-dollars are the main Euro-currency; others include sterling, guilders, Canadian dollars, Deutschemarks, Dutch guilders, French francs, Italian lire, Belgian francs, Japanese yen and Swiss francs. To be used in this way, currencies must be free of rigid restrictions as to their use, and therefore the market has developed since 1958, when the major European currencies were made convertible for non-residents, and exchange control regulations greatly relaxed.

2. A ready market. Euro-currency deposits arise because holders of currency balances, e.g. balances with banks in America, find it profitable to lend them. Eastern European countries were largely responsible for the early development of the Euro-dollar market because they chose to deposit their dollar receipts with banks in Western Europe rather than with banks in the USA.

Until 1970, banks in the United States were prevented from paying interest on deposits held for less than 30 days and the rate that could be paid on longer-term deposits was also limited. Holders of dollars were therefore able to obtain a higher rate of interest by depositing them in Europe instead of the United States. The restrictions did not apply to deposits accepted by branches of American banks outside the United States, so that the US banks were able to obtain dollar deposits by paying comparatively high rates of interest in Europe.

There is a ready market for Euro-dollars and other Euro-currencies. In addition to the demand for dollar balances by the US banks, dollars are also demanded by Continental industrial firms. This has applied particularly at times when interest rates in Britain have been high and the bill on London has been an expensive way of obtaining finance. Banks in Europe also use Euro-currency deposits to finance imports and to make loans to security dealers and brokers in the United States.

Another alternative for the banks is to convert Euro-currency deposits into their own currencies, using the proceeds to make loans in their own money markets at profitable rates of interest. Euro-dollar balances in New York borrowed by a bank in London, for instance, could be sold for sterling and the sterling invested in local government loans or lent to the hire purchase finance houses. When Euro-dollars are converted in this way it is usual for the bank concerned to cover the exchange risk by buying dollars forward to ensure that the dollars are available at the time they are due to be repaid.

The activities of the Euro-currency markets do not increase the supply of foreign currencies, but their effective supply is raised in that the velocity of circulation is increased. It is essential to appreciate that Euro-currencies are currency balances with banks in the country of origin, e.g. Euro-sterling is a balance in sterling with a British bank owned by a non-resident of the UK, and it is a balance which is lent and re-lent in Europe and elsewhere as Euro-sterling.

EURO-CURRENCY QUOTATIONS

3. Uniform rates of interest. The rates of interest paid for deposits of a Euro-currency are fairly uniform from centre to centre, being based on supply and demand for the particular type of deposit (i.e. seven days), in an almost perfect market. London is the leading centre for Euro-dollars and Paris the main centre for Euro-sterling. Quotations for the main Euro-currencies are given in the financial press. The example in Table X has been taken from *The Financial Times*.

Dealers in the market operate on quite low margins, the difference between the rate paid on deposits and that charged on loans being at times as low as $\frac{1}{8}$ per cent.

4. Euro-bonds and Euro-credits. There are links between British banks and banks overseas which enable them jointly to meet the needs of large customers such as multinational companies. These are known as *consortium banks* and their main activity is in the Euro-currency market. Where they extend very large medium-term loans that are sub-participated in by shareholding banks, the loans are referred to as *Euro-credits*. They may be participated in by thirty or forty banks and extend to as much as $1,000 million over ten years.

The consortium banks are also involved in the *Euro-bond* market in which the borrowers are governments or municipal authorities and

TABLE X. EURO-CURRENCY INTEREST RATES

	Sterling	*US dollar*	*Canadian dollar*	*Dutch guilder*	*Swiss franc*
Short term	$12\frac{1}{8}$–$12\frac{3}{8}$	$11\frac{3}{8}$–$11\frac{1}{2}$	$11\frac{1}{4}$–$11\frac{3}{4}$	$6\frac{1}{4}$–$6\frac{3}{8}$	$2\frac{7}{8}$–$3\frac{1}{8}$
7 days' notice	$12\frac{1}{8}$–$12\frac{3}{8}$	$11\frac{5}{16}$–$11\frac{7}{16}$	$11\frac{1}{2}$–12	$6\frac{1}{4}$–$6\frac{3}{8}$	3–$3\frac{1}{4}$
Month	$12\frac{1}{8}$–$12\frac{1}{4}$	$11\frac{7}{16}$–$11\frac{9}{16}$	$12\frac{3}{16}$–$12\frac{3}{8}$	$6\frac{3}{16}$–$6\frac{5}{16}$	$4\frac{9}{16}$–$4\frac{11}{16}$
Three months	$12\frac{7}{16}$–$12\frac{11}{16}$	$11\frac{7}{8}$–12	$12\frac{13}{16}$–13	$6\frac{5}{16}$–$6\frac{7}{16}$	$4\frac{5}{8}$–$4\frac{3}{4}$
Six months	$11\frac{11}{16}$–$11\frac{13}{16}$	$12\frac{1}{2}$–$12\frac{5}{8}$	$13\frac{7}{16}$–$13\frac{5}{8}$	$6\frac{5}{8}$–$6\frac{3}{4}$	$4\frac{3}{4}$–$4\frac{7}{8}$
One year	$11\frac{11}{16}$–$11\frac{13}{16}$	$13\frac{1}{16}$–$13\frac{3}{16}$	$13\frac{11}{16}$–$13\frac{7}{8}$	$6\frac{15}{16}$–$7\frac{1}{16}$	$4\frac{7}{8}$–5

	West German mark	*French franc*	*Italian lira*	*Belgian franc (convertible)*	*Japanese yen*
Short term	$5\frac{1}{4}$–$5\frac{3}{8}$	$11\frac{1}{8}$–$11\frac{3}{8}$	15–16	$11\frac{1}{4}$–$11\frac{3}{4}$	6–$6\frac{1}{8}$
7 days' notice	$5\frac{5}{16}$–$5\frac{7}{16}$	$11\frac{3}{8}$–$11\frac{5}{8}$	$15\frac{3}{8}$–$16\frac{3}{8}$	$11\frac{1}{4}$–$11\frac{3}{4}$	6–$6\frac{1}{8}$
Month	$5\frac{1}{2}$–$5\frac{9}{16}$	$11\frac{3}{8}$–$11\frac{5}{8}$	$15\frac{5}{8}$–$16\frac{1}{8}$	$11\frac{1}{4}$–$11\frac{3}{4}$	$6\frac{1}{16}$–$6\frac{3}{16}$
Three months	$5\frac{13}{16}$–$5\frac{7}{8}$	$11\frac{13}{16}$–$12\frac{1}{16}$	16–$16\frac{1}{2}$	$11\frac{3}{8}$–$11\frac{7}{8}$	$6\frac{1}{4}$–$6\frac{3}{8}$
Six months	$6\frac{1}{4}$–$6\frac{3}{8}$	$12\frac{7}{8}$–$13\frac{1}{8}$	$16\frac{1}{2}$–$16\frac{7}{8}$	$11\frac{1}{2}$–12	$6\frac{3}{8}$–$6\frac{1}{2}$
One year	$6\frac{11}{16}$–$6\frac{3}{4}$	$13\frac{3}{4}$–14	$17\frac{1}{8}$–$17\frac{5}{8}$	$12\frac{3}{8}$–$12\frac{7}{8}$	$6\frac{1}{2}$–$6\frac{5}{8}$

Asian \$ (closing rates in Singapore): Short-term 11–$11\frac{1}{8}$ per cent; seven days' $11\frac{1}{4}$–$11\frac{3}{8}$ per cent; one month $11\frac{1}{2}$–$11\frac{5}{8}$ per cent; three months $11\frac{7}{8}$–12 per cent; six months $12\frac{1}{2}$–$12\frac{5}{8}$ per cent; one year $13\frac{1}{8}$–$13\frac{1}{4}$ per cent. Long-term Euro-dollar: two years $13\frac{3}{4}$–14 per cent; three years $13\frac{1}{8}$–$13\frac{7}{8}$ per cent; four years 14–$14\frac{1}{4}$ per cent; five years 14–$14\frac{1}{4}$ per cent nominal closing rate. Short-term rates are call for US dollars and Japanese yen; others two days' notice.

large firms who require long-term finance of anything from about \$15 million to \$100 million. The bonds are usually advertised in the press and tend to be placed with financial institutions rather than sold to the investing public.

5. Size of the market. Various estimates have been made of the size of the Euro-currency market, but because deposits pass quickly from hand to hand it is difficult to avoid double counting. The Morgan Guaranty Trust Company in its *World Financial Markets* has estimated that gross deposits amounted to £860,000 million in 1978, compared with only £145,000 million in 1971. The majority of the liabilities and claims are in respect of US dollars (about 75–80 per cent).

6. Inter-bank sterling market. This market has existed in London since the early 1960s and is a market in which both resident and non-resident sterling is borrowed and lent, mostly by merchant banks and branches of overseas banks.

PROGRESS TEST 9

1. What is meant by the term Euro-currency? **(1)**
2. When and how did Euro-currencies originate? **(2)**

3. Describe how a bank can borrow a Euro-currency, swap it into its own currency and invest the proceeds covering itself forward. (2)

4. Why are Euro-currencies quoted as rates of interest and not as rates of exchange? (3)

5. What is meant by the term consortium bank? (4)

6. What are Euro-credits and Euro-bonds? (4)

CHAPTER X

Exchange Arithmetic

THE NEED FOR ACCURACY

1. Accuracy. Foreign exchange calculations should not present an insuperable problem once the methods employed have been fully understood, for they involve nothing more than an ability to multiply, divide, add and subtract correctly. The need for accuracy in foreign exchange calculations cannot be stressed too strongly. A small margin of error of (say) 2 per cent in calculating a fraction or decimal of a currency unit which is to be multiplied may seem insignificant. It still remains an error of 2 per cent, however, when it is multiplied and if it is to be multiplied by a large number then the error becomes 2 per cent of a large amount and is significant.

It is always as well to check your calculations as you proceed, and a very rough calculation in advance as to what the final answer should be will make you recheck your work if your answer is very different from the estimate. This rough check is particularly desirable where decimal sums are involved as it is so easy to put the decimal point in the wrong place. Furthermore, if a rough estimate is prepared, all the noughts to the right of the last digit in a number can be ignored when using a calculator, e.g. a rough estimate gives £30, therefore:

$$£\frac{30,400 \times 9 \times 4}{100 \times 365}$$

can be put into the calculator as:

$$£\frac{304 \times 9 \times 4}{365}$$

$$= £\frac{10,944}{365}$$

$$= £\ 299,835 \text{ (ignoring the decimal point)}$$
$$= £\ 29.98$$

(*see* Example 1 *below*).

Decimals are invaluable for foreign exchange calculations as they save time and effort, but they can give incorrect answers unless amounts are taken to several decimal places. Where a decimal is to be multiplied by a large number and the decimal does not work out exactly, then it must be taken to at least five decimal places before it is multiplied. Answers should always be given to the nearest currency unit, for instance, £17.527 = £17.53.

2. Neatness. In presenting arithmetic answers, neatness and style are important. The steps in the calculation should be shown clearly especially if a calculator is used and hence all the arithmetic is not shown. Even if your answer is incorrect, you will gain marks if you have used the right method and have worked neatly, so make the steps that you have taken perfectly clear to the examiner.

3. Fractions into decimals. Some foreign exchange quotations are still expressed in fractions, but it is a fairly easy matter to convert them into decimals. The following conversions should be memorised. Expressed as decimals:

$$\frac{3}{4} = 0.75$$
$$\frac{1}{2} = 0.5$$
$$\frac{1}{4} = 0.25$$
$$\frac{1}{8} = 0.125$$
$$\frac{1}{16} = 0.0625$$

From these decimals all fractions that are multiples of $\frac{1}{16}$th, i.e. from $\frac{1}{16}$th to $\frac{15}{16}$th, can be calculated.

INTEREST, COMMISSION, PREMIUMS AND DISCOUNTS

4. Calculation of interest. Where it is necessary to calculate interest in foreign exchange questions, the following formula should be used:

$$I = \frac{P \times R \times N}{100 \times 365}$$

where I = interest, P = principal, R = rate per annum, and N = number of days.

EXAMPLE 1

Find the interest on £30,400 for 9 days at 4 per cent per annum.

$$Rough\ estimate: \quad £\frac{30,000 \times 9 \times 4}{100 \times 360} = £\frac{3,000}{100} = £30$$

Solution: $£\dfrac{30,400 \times 9 \times 4}{100 \times 365} = £\dfrac{10,944}{365} = £299,835$

From the rough answer it can be seen that the answer is £29.98.

5. Banker's commission and expenses. When buying or selling a currency a banker may charge a commission which is calculated on the sterling amount. This varies, but may, for instance, be $1\frac{1}{2}$ per mille, with a maximum of £15. On a purchase of a foreign currency the bank's commission must be deducted from the sterling amount and where currency is sold by the bank the commission must be added. Any expenses involved, such as stamp duty and postage, must be added or deducted from the sterling amount in the same way. In an examination question guidance will always be given as to the scale of commission to use and what other charges to allow for.

6. Discounts and premiums as an annual percentage rate. Forward premiums and discounts are closely related to international interest rates, and foreign exchange transactions may become worth while if there is a gap (frequently referred to as the *differential*) between them and the rates of interest. The student must therefore be able to express quickly premiums and discounts as an annual percentage rate.

The premium (or discount) must first be multiplied by 12 if it is a one-month premium, or by 4 if it is for three months, in order to express it as an annual premium. It is then expressed as a fraction of the forward rate and the fraction needs to be multiplied by 100 to convert it into a percentage.

EXAMPLE 2

What is the cost of covering forward, expressed as an annual percentage rate, when the one-month discount is 0.72 cents and the spot rate is $2.6095 = £1?

The annual rate of discount is $0.72 \times 12 = 8.64$ cents.

The discount is given in cents *not* per cent and to express it as a fraction of the forward rate the latter must be converted into cents.

Forward rate = 2.6095 + 0.72 cents = 2.6167 = 261.67 cents.

$$\therefore \quad \frac{8.64}{261.67} \times 100 = \frac{864}{261.67} = 3.3 \text{ per cent.}$$

Such an accurate calculation would not be necessary unless it was clearly indicated in the question. If, for instance, the question asked "show how this is approximately 3% per annum," then it would be safe to round off the figures and simplify the calculations as follows:

8.64 cents = 9 cents approx.
Forward rate is $2.62 approx.

$$\frac{9}{262} \times 100 = \frac{100}{29} = 3 \text{ per cent approx.}$$

THE SUM IN STERLING

Examination questions on forward exchange frequently require the candidate, in addition to selecting the appropriate rate, to calculate the sum in sterling which will be debited or credited to the customer's account. The technique involved in deciding the right rate of exchange to use has already been described in detail in VII. The following notes are mostly concerned with the arithmetic involved in calculating the sterling sum.

Arithmetical questions are designed to test the candidate's ability to apply principles to practice. They are often long and unnecessarily detailed, but do not be distracted by this. For instance, a question may contain quotations for both spot and forward rates for two currencies when, in fact, only a spot quotation is necessary for one and a forward rate for the other, but the examiner is trying to test your ability to decide what is required. Look at the question and ask yourself "What amounts of foreign currency are to be paid or received, and when?" Some simple calculations may be involved here, such as multiplying the price per tonne by the number of tonnes being bought or sold, but such sums should cause no difficulty.

Study the following typical questions, and solutions, very carefully and try to work them out independently (several times if necessary, until you have mastered the technique). Further arithmetical problems will be found in Progress Test 10.

NOTE: The exchange rates used in these questions are not a true reflection of the rates for these currencies at the time of preparing this edition.

SPECIMEN QUESTION 1

On 1st January a customer notifies his bank that he has entered into a contract to buy 200,000 sparking plugs from Milan at 88 lire each c.i.f., payment to be made immediately. He has also signed a contract to sell the sparking plugs to a US buyer for $35,000 for settlement during March.

The customer instructs his bank to pay the lire immediately by mail transfer and to buy the dollars forward.

On 1st January the quotations for Italian lire and US dollars are as follows:

	Italian lire	US dollars
Spot	1,502–3	2.5917–5927
One month forward	5–4 l. pm	0.15–0.05 c. pm
Two months forward	7½–6½ l. pm	0.45–0.35 c. pm
Three months forward	10–9 l. pm	0.75–0.65 c. pm

The mail transfer commission charged to the customer is ⅛ per cent and exchange commission is charged at 1 per mille with a maximum of £10.

When the two foreign exchange transactions are complete, what amounts will be debited and credited to the customer's account?

ANSWER

What amounts of foreign currency are to be paid or received, and when?
A mail transfer for 200,000 × 88 lire = 17,600,000 lire is to be sent immediately and $35,000 will be received some time in March.

The lire will cost $\dfrac{17,600,000}{1,502}$

Rough estimate: 17,500,000 ÷ 1,500 = £11,700

$$1,502 \overline{\smash)17,600,000} \quad 11,717.709$$

	= £11,717.71
Mail transfer commission: ⅛ per cent	14.65
Exchange commission: 1 per mille, max. £10	10.00
Amount debited to customer	= £11,742.36

The bank buying the US dollars will want as many as possible for each £1. These dollars are to be sold forward to the bank as they will not be received until March, and as the forward dollar is at a premium which *must be deducted* from the spot rate the bank will want to deduct the smallest premium possible. The earliest date on which the dollars will be received is 1st March which is two months forward so that the premium will be 0.45–0.35 c. The buying rate will therefore be:

$$\begin{array}{r} \$2.5927 \\ 35 \\ \hline \$2.5892 \end{array}$$

A rough estimate of the sterling sum is $35,000 \div 2.5 = £14,000$

$$\begin{array}{r} 13,517.69 \\ 2.5892 \overline{)35,000} \end{array}$$

	$= £13,517.69$
Less 1 per mille commission, max. £10	10.00
Amount to be credited	$= £13,507.69$

SPECIMEN QUESTION 2

On 1st June a British merchant purchases machine tools from West Germany for DM 144,200 and resells them on three-month credit terms for DM 197,200.

In order to pay for his purchase at once it is necessary for him to borrow in London at 6 per cent per annum. He has the alternative of taking three months' credit from his German supplier for which he will add $5\frac{1}{2}$ per cent per annum to his invoice.

Exchange quotations on 1st June are as follows:

| Spot | DM 8.30$\frac{3}{4}$–31$\frac{1}{4}$ |
| 3 months forward | 9–8$\frac{3}{4}$ pf. pm. |

Allowing for exchange commission at 1 per mille, maximum £10, which is the cheaper way of financing the deal and what will be his net profit in sterling?

ANSWER

The British merchant would find it cheaper to pay for his purchase at once because although he could borrow at $\frac{1}{2}$ per cent cheaper in Germany, in doing so he would deny himself the benefit of buying D.marks spot and selling them forward at a premium. The premium is equivalent to considerably more than $\frac{1}{2}$ per cent—at approx. 0.09 marks for three months on each 8.23 marks (the forward rate of 8.31$\frac{3}{4}$–8$\frac{3}{4}$) this works out at

$$\frac{0.09 \times 4 \times 100}{8.23} = \frac{36}{8.23} = 4 \text{ per cent approx.}$$

He will therefore remit DM 144,200 on 1st June, pay interest at 6 per cent per annum for three months on the sterling sum, and sell DM 197,200 three months forward.

DM 144,200 at 8.30¾ would cost him approximately 144,000/8 = £18,000.

$$\begin{array}{r} 17,357.809 \\ \hline 83,075)\overline{144,200} \end{array}$$

	= £17,357.81
Plus exchange commission 1 per mille, max. £10	10.00
	£17,367.81

The rate of exchange for the forward sale of DM 197,200 would be:

$$8.31¾ - 8¾ = 8.23$$

This would yield approximately 200,000/8 = £25,000.

$$\begin{array}{r} 23,961.117 \\ \hline 823)\overline{197,200} \end{array}$$

	= £23,961.12
Less exchange commission 1 per mille, max. £10	10.00
	£23,951.12

Three months from 1st June would be 1st September, which is 92 days. The interest on £17,367.81 for the period would therefore be:

$$\frac{17,367.81 \times 92 \times 6}{100 \times 365}$$

Rough estimate: $£\dfrac{17,000}{100} \times \dfrac{1}{4} \times \dfrac{6}{1} = \dfrac{1,020}{4} = £255$

$$\frac{17,367.81 \times 92 \times 6}{100 \times 365} = \frac{9,587,031}{365} = 262,658$$

By reference to the rough estimate we can see that the answer is £262.66.

The profit on the transactions would therefore be:

		£23,951.12
Less £17,367.81		
262.66		£17,630.47
	Answer	£6,320.65

SPECIMEN QUESTION 3

A British importer contracts to purchase from a French manufacturer 50 dozen pairs of ladies' fashion boots at a cost of Fr. 1,195.20 per dozen. Despatch is to be by air-freight in two separate consignments of 25 dozen pairs (one in January and one in February), and payment is to be made immediately upon receipt of telex advice of despatch. On 1st January, the importer requests his bank to cover him forward for these transactions.

While the first consignment arrives safely and is paid for on 25th January, the second is delayed by industrial action, with the result that delivery cannot take place until some time in March. The importer arranges for his bank to extend the contract, and the goods are eventually depatched on 20th March.

On the basis of the rates quoted below and exchange commission of 1 per mille, maximum £10 (but charging only $\frac{1}{2}$ per mille, maximum £10, on the extension) calculate the total sterling amount paid by the importer.

	1st January	1st March
Spot	13.34$\frac{1}{2}$–13.35	13.35$\frac{1}{2}$–13.36
1 month	4$\frac{1}{2}$–3$\frac{3}{4}$c prem	5–4$\frac{1}{4}$c prem
2 months	6$\frac{1}{2}$–5$\frac{3}{4}$c prem	7–6$\frac{1}{4}$c prem
3 months	8$\frac{1}{2}$–7$\frac{3}{4}$c prem	9–8$\frac{1}{4}$c prem

ANSWER

The importer will have to pay Fr. 1,195.20 × 25 = 29,880 during January, i.e. one-month forward option, and a similar amount in February, i.e. two-month forward option over second month. He will enter into a contract with the bank to buy these at Fr. 13.30 and Fr. 13.28 = £1 respectively. The basis used in calculating these rates is as follows.

The first payment will have to be made at any time during January, and therefore the bank will assume that it will occur at the least favourable time of the month from the customer's point of view. This will be on the last day (one month forward from 1st January). The bank will wish to supply as few francs for each £1 as possible, so therefore will pay 13.34½ less 4½ premium. Likewise for the second contract it will pay out as few francs as possible and will use the rate for two months forward, i.e. 13.34½ less 6½ premium, rather than the rate at the beginning of the option period.

To complete the contract on 1st March (the end of the second option period), the customer sells the temporarily unwanted francs back at the spot rate of 13.36. He extends for one month his option to purchase francs and will be quoted the close-out rate 13.36 less the selling margin for one month (5 cents) = 13.31.

The reader is referred back to VIII, 8, where the principles involved in calculating the rate of exchange for an extension are explained.

The calculations involved are as follows:

Fr. 29,880 at 13.30

Rough estimate of cost $= \dfrac{30,000}{13} = £2,300$ approx.

$$\dfrac{29,880}{1,330} = 2,246.62$$

Add exchange commission   2.25

£2,248.87

Fr. 29,880 at 13.28 $= £2,300$ approx.

$$\dfrac{29,880}{1,328} = 2,250.00$$

Add exchange commission   2.25

£2,252.25

Fr. 29,880 at 13.36 $= £2,300$ approx.

$$\dfrac{29,880}{1,336} = £2,236.53$$

∴ Customer debited with   £2,252.25

Less   2,236.53

$= £ \quad 15.72$

Extension
Fr. 29,880 at 13.31   = £2,300 approx.

$$\frac{29,880}{1,331} = £2,244.93$$

Add exchange commission at
 ½ per mille   1.12
                                                   ─────────
                                                   £2,246.05
                                                   ─────────

∴ *Importer will have to pay*   £2,248.87
                                          15.72
                                       2,246.05
                                       ─────────
                                       £4,510.64
                                       ═════════

PROGRESS TEST 10
(Exchange arithmetic questions)

Do not refer to the answers to the questions (which are given in Appendix VI) until you have attempted all the questions in a section. If some of your answers are wrong, rework the questions in the section, several times if necessary, until you can answer all of them speedily and accurately.

1. Convert into decimals (3):

(a) ¾   (d) ⅝
(b) ⅜   (e) ⅛
(c) ¼   (f) ⅞

2. Calculate the following (4):

(a) What is the interest on £749.12 for 11 days at 5 per cent per annum?

(b) What is the interest on £30,881 for 12 days at 7 per cent?

(c) What is the interest on £40,000 for 72 days at 4 per cent?

(d) What is the interest, in dollars, on $375.2 for 82 days at 5 per cent?

3. On 1st September, a London merchant agrees to buy two drilling machines from the USA, one for $16,000 and the other for $11,500. The first ($16,000) is to be shipped during September and the other not later than 31st October. Payment in each case is to be made by cable transfer immediately on shipment.

The merchant resells the machines on the same day to a Dutch buyer for 64,000 guilders and 46,000 guilders respectively and the two machines are to be sent direct from the USA to Holland c.i.f. Payment is to be received one month after shipment.

The merchant arranges the necessary forward exchange with his bank. The rates of exchange on 1st September are as follows:

	$	Guilders
Spot	2.6117–6127	$8.39\frac{3}{4}$–$8.40\frac{3}{4}$
1 month forward	0.15–0.05	$3\frac{3}{8}$–$3\frac{1}{8}$ c. pm
2 months forward	0.45–0.35 c. pm	$6\frac{3}{8}$–$6\frac{1}{8}$ c. pm
3 months forward	0.75–0.65 c. pm	$8\frac{3}{4}$–$8\frac{1}{2}$ c. pm

Exchange commission is 1 per mille, maximum £10. How much profit does he make on the transaction?

4. On 1st January, a London importer signs a contract with a Canadian fur dealer to supply skins at $4.05 each c.i.f. London.

Shipments are to be made as follows:

> 1,000 skins during January
> 3,000 skins during January–February
> 2,500 skins during February–March.

Payment is to be made by cable on receipt of advice of shipment. The importer arranges forward exchange on 1st January, the rates being as follows on that date:

Spot	$2.5850–5870
1 month forward	0.45–0.25 c. pm
2 months forward	0.65–0.45 c. pm
3 months forward	0.85–0.65 c. pm

Shipments are actually made as follows:

> 9th January   1,000 skins
> 1st March   3,000 skins
> 31st March   2,900 skins

The importer agrees to pay for the excess shipment.

The spot rate on 31st March is $2.5825–5845.

What amounts are debited by the bank to the merchant's account? Allow for exchange commission at 1 per mille on each contract with a maximum of £10.

PART THREE

DEVELOPMENT OF OVERSEAS TRADE

CHAPTER XI

Banking Facilities

FINDING A BUYER OR SELLER

1. Business opportunities. To the British manufacturer or merchant who proposes to enter into international trade as either an exporter or an importer, the banking system (i.e. both the clearing and merchant banks) provides a source from which he can obtain a great deal of help and advice as to the opportunities for his particular type of business.

The banks are able to provide their customers with the names of possible buyers and sellers and agents and distributors of goods in all parts of the world as well as names and addresses of firms and organisations which may be interested in linking with a British company in some joint venture overseas. Furthermore, the banks maintain registers of UK importers and exporters covering every branch of trade and industry and are thus able to direct business enquiries received from overseas correspondent banks to those customers who may be interested in the opportunities offered.

2. Introductions. The best way of establishing or developing a market overseas is for the trader to visit the market, to study the particular requirements of that country (e.g. the packaging and advertising techniques adopted) and to make personal contact with existing and potential customers. In this connection, the banks are able to provide introductions through their correspondent banks overseas, from which the customer is able to obtain on-the-spot help and advice once he has arrived in the country concerned.

In addition, the banks do, of course, provide the facilities for financing journeys abroad such as traveller's cheques, letters of credit and supplies of foreign currencies.

3. Trade development departments. In recent years, the larger banks have established sections or departments charged with the responsibility of trade development. Officers in these departments travel extensively around the world collecting information on trade prospects, and are in a position to advise customers from their own personal experience about the markets in which they are interested.

In addition to their correspondents overseas, the banks are able to give introductions or advice through the medium of their own overseas subsidiary banks and through the banking groups with which they are associated.

SERVICES FOR THE IMPORTER

4. Paying for imports. The importer can arrange through his bank to pay for the goods which he has imported, in accordance with the terms of his contract. If he has agreed to open a documentary credit in the seller's favour then he can instruct his bank to open it through a correspondent bank in the exporter's country. Alternatively, if it is agreed that the seller shall draw a sight or term bill on the importer, the exporter may be able to negotiate it or, more probably, would send it through his bank for collection.

Other methods of payment, such as mail and telegraphic transfers and drafts, are, of course, available through the banking system.

Where payments are to be made in a foreign currency at some future date, the importer can enter into a forward exchange contract with his bank to purchase the currency when required at a rate to be determined immediately.

5. Obtaining finance. If the exporter agrees to draw a usance bill under a documentary credit opened by the importer's bank, the importer has a period of time in which to resell the goods before having to pay for them. Foreign exporters like the benefit of such a documentary acceptance credit of a London bank because they are enabled to draw bills on London which are readily negotiable.

Where the foreign exporter insists on drawing a sight draft instead of a usance draft, the importer may be able to obtain finance from a commercial bank by way of a *merchandise advance* or a merchant bank by way of a *reimbursement draft*. A merchandise advance is a loan on the security of the goods which the importer has purchased and it enables him to pay for the goods. A reimbursement draft is one drawn on a merchant bank which will be accepted by the bank so that it can then be discounted as a bank bill in the London market. The merchant bank thus lends its name to enable the importer to obtain finance but does, of course, run the risk that the importer will not have paid in the proceeds from the resale of the goods before the bill matures. Whether the finance is obtained from a clearing bank or a merchant bank, the bank will probably insist on having control of the shipping documents as security. The importer may be allowed to take possession of the documents temporarily so as to deliver the goods to the buyer, but will be required to sign a *Trust Receipt* and thus pledge himself to act as agent and trustee for the bank in dealing with the goods.

6. Suppliers of goods. It has already been mentioned how the banks can help importers to find foreign suppliers of the goods they wish to buy. In addition, the banks can supply status reports on the suppliers as to their creditworthiness and ability to fulfil the contracts into which they have entered.

SERVICES FOR THE EXPORTER

7. Opportunities. The ways in which the banks provide information about business opportunities have already been mentioned, but one further facility for the exporter needs to be considered under this heading. We have so far taken it for granted that the exporter knows which countries offer him the best opportunities and, thus having narrowed the field, he can try to find buyers in those countries. If, however, he has no idea which are the best markets, the banks, through their intelligence departments and overseas branches, are able to provide trade statistics from which it is fairly clear which markets have shown the most rapid rate of expansion. Furthermore, through their correspondents they are able to make enquiries about the potential demand for particular products.

8. Economic and political reports. Closely allied to the market demand for a particular product is the economic and political situation in a country. A country which is politically and economically unstable is obviously a risky market. Therefore an exporter who intends to trade extensively with importers in a country about which he knows only little would probably wish to avail himself of the facility whereby the banks will provide a report on the situation in any particular country. A report which shows that a country's balance of payments is seriously adverse would suggest the danger of import restrictions which may preclude an importer from fulfilling his contract with a British exporter. Political unrest, too, disrupts trade and payments, and makes trading with the country concerned more risky. Such risks resulting from economic and political instability can be insured against through the Export Credits Guarantee Department and, on receiving a report from a bank pointing out the instability, an exporter would probably be more inclined to make use of ECGD.

9. Status enquiries. After deciding on the best markets for his goods and having found buyers in them, the exporter can make enquiries through his bank as to the creditworthiness and reliability of the importers concerned. The banks maintain status reports on many hundreds of thousands of firms and individuals both at home and abroad, and if they are unable to produce a report on a particular foreign trader from their records they can quickly obtain one by Telex or cable to one of their correspondent banks overseas. The customer can repeat his enquiry about a buyer of his goods every year (or even six months) in order to satisfy himself that the buyer's creditworthiness has not deteriorated.

10. Methods of payment. The methods by which the exporter can obtain payment for his goods have already been described in detail in II, IV and V, and quite obviously facilitating payments is one of the most important services which the banks provide for the exporter. The method of payment to be used must be clearly defined in the exporter's contract with his buyer and he must also ensure that there is no doubt as to who is to pay the expenses of freight and insurance. If the contract stipulates that the goods are to be supplied f.o.b. (free on board) then the exporter is responsible for getting the goods on to the ship and they are the buyer's responsibility after that. If, on the other hand, the contract is a c.i.f. (cost, insurance, freight) contract, then the seller is responsible for insuring the goods as well as for paying the freight charges.

Where an exporter is in any doubt as to the method of payment to insist on, his bank will advise him. As has already been explained, the best arrangement is a confirmed irrevocable documentary credit, which will ensure that he receives payment on delivering the documents to his bank or within a stipulated period thereafter. However, sellers' markets have disappeared and he may have to be content with a less satisfactory means of payment. There are customary forms of payment for trade in some commodities and also trade with particular areas, and an exporter may have no alternative but to accept them.

Foreign currency receipts can be sold in advance through the forward exchange market at a rate of exchange fixed immediately.

11. Trade and exchange restrictions. The banks are able to obtain information about restrictions on trade and payments imposed by governments overseas. These can take the form of tariffs and quotas and exchange control restrictions. The British exporter must not assume that because a foreign importer has an import licence it implies automatic authority to acquire the necessary foreign exchange.

Restrictions may be imposed at short notice which may prevent the purchaser from importing the goods even though he has contracted to buy them or to pay for goods that have been imported. A British exporter may, therefore, find himself with goods for which there is no market or with frozen debts in a foreign currency. These risks can, of course, be insured against through Export Credits Guarantee Department but, for the exporter who has not covered himself in this way, consultation with his bank about trade and exchange restrictions may save him from loss.

12. Contracts with foreign governments. Where an exporter tenders for a contract with a foreign government or municipal authority he may have to provide a *tender guarantee* for a small percentage of the amount of the contract. If he succeeds in obtaining the contract, he may then have to replace the tender guarantee with a *performance guarantee* or *bond* for a larger percentage (possibly 5–10 per cent of the amount of the contract). These guarantees must usually be issued by a bank in the foreign country concerned and can be arranged with the exporter's bank through a correspondent bank overseas.

13. Post-shipment finance. (NOTE: *The appropriate parts of XIII on the work of the Export Credits Guarantee Department must be carefully read in conjunction with this section.*)

To enable the exporter to give extended credit to his buyer, the banks provide post-shipment finance.

The British banks have provided an ever-increasing amount of this type of finance as competition has developed and exporters have been forced to offer extended credit terms in order to gain business. Much of it has been provided by the banks against a lien on the exporter's ordinary ECGD comprehensive guarantee, but the banks would not have been able to provide anywhere near as much export finance if the Department had not introduced in 1954 the *Specific Bank Guarantee,* and in 1966 and 1967 the bill guarantee (*Comprehensive Bill Guarantee*) and the open account guarantee (*Comprehensive Open Account Guarantee*) respectively, which give a bank a direct and unconditional guarantee against the risks which are inherent in providing credit for exporters (*see* XIII, **16, 17, 25**). In some countries special government-sponsored financial institutions have been established to meet the growing need for post-shipment finance, but in the UK there is no such institution and the banks have provided the necessary finance.

The race to compete in credit terms has caused countries some concern, for it has been realised that not only does the provision of credit to an overseas buyer represent a strain upon the balance of payments and currency of the country exporting the goods, but also, if the race gets out of hand, only the foreign importer will benefit. Because of this, the Berne Union (an association of credit insurers, including ECGD) has tried to restrict credit to five years. The credit insurers agreed not to provide export insurance when credit terms exceeded this period except under special circumstances, and to a considerable extent the five-year period has been adhered to, despite the pressure for longer-term credit.

Where a British exporter sells capital goods on up to five-years' credit (or possibly more), he obtains an ECGD bank guarantee and usually draws bills of exchange or receives promissory notes in a series payable at six-monthly intervals. Normally these cover principal and interest in equal instalments. They are lodged with his bank for presentation when they fall due and if they are not paid within three months of due date the bank claims against ECGD within the terms of the bank guarantee.

The banks charge a fixed rate of interest per annum for export finance against bank guarantees and the difference, if any, between this rate and the market rate of interest for loans of a similar term is made up by a government subsidy to the banks.

14. Bill finance. There are three ways by which an exporter of consumer goods can obtain finance from a bank on the strength of a bill drawn on the importer:

(*a*) by negotiating the draft with a clearing bank or merchant bank;

(*b*) by using the draft as security for an overdraft of possibly 85 or 90 per cent of its face value (or 100 per cent if there is an ECGD bill guarantee);

(*c*) by obtaining an *acceptance credit* from a merchant bank for a proportion of the face value of the bill. The exporter hands the bill to the bank for collection and then draws a bill on the bank as provided for in the credit. The merchant bank accepts this second bill and the exporter then has a bank bill which he can discount in the London market.

The bill on the importer is taken by the bank before it is accepted and, whichever method is used, the bank will retain recourse against its customer and will hold the draft as its primary security. If the bank holds an ECGD bill guarantee it will retain recourse against the customer only until the bill has been accepted.

MEDIUM- AND LONG-TERM EXPORT CREDIT

NOTE: *The appropriate parts of XIII on the work of the Export Credits Guarantee Department must be carefully read in conjunction with this section.*

15. Direct loans to buyers. For contracts concerned with heavy capital equipment and ships, credit up to and beyond a five-year period is frequently required which, under normal circumstances, would be beyond the commercial banks' resources. Competition from overseas has been so keen in recent years, however, that ways and means have had to be found to enable British suppliers to compete in the credit race.

In 1960, the Export Credits Guarantee Department started to give insurance cover for credit extended over longer periods than five years where it could be shown that similar terms were being offered by foreign suppliers who were backed by credit insurers. In the following year the Department introduced *financial guarantees* which subsequently became known as *buyer credit guarantees*, which cover loans made by a bank or other financial institution *direct to an overseas buyer*. This is quite distinct from the post-shipment finance referred to in **7–14** above, which is finance *by the seller* to the buyer on the strength of loans made to the seller by a bank or other financial institution.

16. Buyer credit guarantees. ECGD buyer credit guarantees (*see* XIII, **26–8**) enable the supplier to be paid in cash even though the buyer requires credit of two years or more.

Normally only contracts for £1,000,000 or more will be considered for this type of guarantee and ECGD must be satisfied that it is clearly in the interest of the UK to provide the facility to the overseas buyer. The buyer must provide at least 15–20 per cent of the purchase price.

It is the responsibility of the UK supplier to find the source of finance for the overseas buyer and to arrange for the financial guarantee and pay the premium to ECGD.

17. Bank of England re-financing. The extent to which the banks in the post-war years provided medium- and long-term finance for export resulted in a strain upon their liquidity position. In order to overcome this, the Bank of England made various arrangements whereby the banks could obtain re-finance facilities if they wished, i.e. they could sell some of the export loans to the Bank of England. However, these facilities no longer apply, though when agreeing in 1980 to provide all the export credit required without this type of backing the banks were given assurances that in a real emergency some of these loans would be re-financed.

18. Forfaiting. This is a method of providing medium-term finance for exporters which is becoming increasingly popular where trade between the UK and the Continent is involved. Where the seller has drawn a series of bills of exchange on the buyer (or the buyer has given the seller a series of promissory notes) a bank may be prepared to forfait them. It may on occasions be willing to apply the practice to guaranteed book debt obligations where bills or notes are not available.

In effect the bank negotiates the bills or notes on a non-recourse basis but it will invariably require that the bills or notes are *avalised*. This is the term applied to a guarantee by the importer's bank that the bills or notes will be paid. Such a guarantee is referred to as an *aval*.

An important advantage to the exporter is that his bank will usually commit itself in advance to negotiate the bills at a rate agreed at the outset plus a commitment fee. The exporter is therefore able to work out what his proceeds will be and he can base his price to the buyer on what these will amount to. He is likely to be able to offer the best possible terms to the overseas buyer knowing that he need not be cautious and make provision for erosion of the proceeds from changes in interest rates or in the other expenses of obtaining finance because these factors have been taken care of by the forfaiting process. He gets immediate cash for his exports and is relieved of liability as there is no recourse. He is relieved of the chore of having to present the bills as they fall due and his overdraft facilities are left available for use in other parts of his business.

PROGRESS TEST 11

1. What services does a bank provide for importers? **(4–6)**

2. List the ways in which a bank can be of assistance to an exporter. **(7–14)**

3. What is meant by post-shipment finance? What is its main source of supply in Britain? **(14)**

4. In what ways can an exporter obtain finance on the strength of a bill drawn on an importer? **(14)**

5. Summarise the developments in the provision of long-term export cr it in the UK in recent years. **(15–18)**

  What is meant by re-finance facilities? **(17)**

  xplain the process of forfaiting. **(18)**

CHAPTER XII

Other Services to Exporters

NOTE: Justice cannot be done in this chapter to all the firms and institutions in the UK that provide services to exporters. Those that are mentioned constitute only a representative sample to give the student a broad outline of the services and expertise available.

THE BRITISH OVERSEAS TRADE BOARD

1. Export promotion services. The Board, which consists of businessmen and representatives from the Department of Trade and Industry and the Foreign and Commonwealth Office, offers a wide range of services both to the importer and to the exporter. For the exporter these services include the following:

(a) guidance on individual export problems;
(b) information on the most likely market for a product;
(c) introductions to potential agents and buyers;
(d) help with overseas business visits;
(e) status reports on foreign firms;
(f) information on tariff and import regulations;
(g) details of overseas contracts out for tender;
(h) help and advice on participating in trade fairs overseas;
(i) assistance in finding a licensee to manufacture a product abroad;
(j) advice on marketing and advertising a product abroad;
(k) investigation into product suitability for foreign tastes.

Most of these services are self-explanatory, but the following points about them should be noted.

(a) *Locating markets.* With the help of their officials overseas, the Department of Trade and Industry and the Foreign and Commonwealth Office are able to supply information about business conditions, local production and imports, competition, and local tastes and trading methods.

(b) *Overseas business visits.* Through commercial officers and trade commissioners it is possible for the Department of Trade and Industry to make introductions and appointments and collect information for the exporter before he arrives in the country concerned. Local publicity can often be arranged.

(c) *Status reports.* These are concerned with the standing of the potential importer or agent, not with his creditworthiness. Reports on the latter are obtainable through a bank or credit reporting agency.

(d) *Tariffs and import regulations.* The information obtainable includes details of regulations concerning certificates of origin, consular invoices and fees, trade and merchandise marks and imports of samples.

(e) *Contracts for tender.* Particulars of contracts put out to tender by overseas governments, municipalities and similar bodies are published in *Export Intelligence Service* which is obtainable by subscription. This service also provides information about export opportunities, market reports and pointers, and news about the economic position and business climate in overseas markets. Similar information is published in the weekly journal *British Industry.*

(f) *Market entry guarantee scheme.* The BOTB runs the scheme to help small manufacturers cope with the financial risks involved in breaking into an overseas market. The Board provides half the costs which it recoups by a levy on sales receipts. If a venture is unsuccessful half the loss is borne by the BOTB.

FACTORING

2. Functions of a factor. In the last twenty years factoring organisations, offering a comprehensive service, have been established in Britain and the British banks have set up or acquired subsidiary companies offering these services.

The functions of a factoring house are as follows:

(a) to give the seller 100 per cent credit insurance by taking over his invoices as the goods are supplied and collecting payment *without recourse;*

(b) to provide a complete sales accounting service;

(c) to provide cash either immediately or at an agreed future date for the full face-value of the invoices less the factor's charges;

(d) in addition, the factoring house may offer to secure overseas buyers and agents, and obtain status reports.

3. How factoring is organised. Factoring organisations have overseas branches through which arrangements can be made for the collection of payments. They have close links with banks, or are owned by them, and through them are able to present bills of exchange and similar credit instruments for payment. Status reports are also obtained through this medium.

On the basis of status reports, factoring houses set a limit for each overseas buyer, and the exporter can supply his goods up to this limit and submit his invoice to the factor.

The most common form of factoring is disclosed factoring, i.e. the factor's name is disclosed to the buyer. It is usual for the factoring house to insist on its name being disclosed to the buyer. This is to be expected in view of the fact that the factoring house buys the debt without recourse and is better able to collect the debt in its own name than in that of the seller. However, it is possible to arrange with a factoring house for undisclosed factoring where the business is conducted entirely in the name of the company selling the goods. Another possibility is straight-forward invoice discounting where the sales ledger remains in the control of the seller.

4. Advantages to the seller. To the exporting firm which is short of working capital, factoring provides additional capital, for the item "Sundry debtors" in its balance sheet becomes "Cash" if the factor provides immediate payment for the goods sold. This may enable the firm to expand its output and benefit from the economies of scale. Furthermore, by making prompt payment for raw materials and other purchases, the firm is able to secure better terms from its suppliers.

There may be less need, too, for bank finance; but it might be cheaper to continue to borrow from a bank and employ the factor simply for sales accounting and the collection of remittances, payments being made by the factor not immediately but after an interval of time. Where a factoring house is to make immediate payments to the exporter its charges will be higher because it must base its charges on the fact that it may itself have to borrow from a bank in order to pay the seller upon receipt of the invoices and will not receive payments from the buyers for some time thereafter.

Another advantage to the seller is that having been relieved of the problem of sales accounting and the collection of payments, the management can devote more time to other aspects of the business.

EXPORT HOUSES

5. Confirming houses. Some firms in the UK which act as agents for foreign importers have become established as *confirming houses* (sometimes known as *indent houses*). As such, their functions are:

(*a*) to receive indents from foreign importers ordering particular types of goods and possibly naming the particular brand required;

(*b*) to pass on the indents to manufacturers;

(*c*) to add their confirmation to the orders, i.e. to assume responsibility for the debt;

(*d*) to receive the goods from the manufacturer and arrange for shipping.

The advantages to the manufacturer are that he is assured of payment when the goods are despatched and he has the confirming house near at hand to consult concerning quality and packaging requirements, etc.

6. Other export houses. There is a wide variety of types of export house offering expertise in marketing particular types of goods and on the methods of trading in individual markets. The distinction between an export house and a confirming house is that the export house is the *exporter's* agent, whereas the confirming house is the *importer's* agent. Instead of acting as agent, an export house may buy the manufacturer's goods and sell them at a profit. They usually take over the packing, shipping and insurance of the goods and may assist in establishing a network of distributors for the goods overseas.

CREDIT TO THE IMPORTER

7. Credit unions. As an alternative to borrowing himself and allowing the importer time to pay, the exporter can arrange for a credit to be made available to the importer. One way of doing this is through one of the international credit unions. In recent years, the British banks and other financial institutions have forged very close links with banks and finance houses abroad, especially in Europe, and through these links are able to offer a wide range of services to their customers.

The members of the organisations provide credit for the importers of a wide range of vehicles, capital goods and some kinds of domestic equipment. The British exporter notifies the British finance house or bank that is a member of that credit union of the name of the importer and details of his credit requirements, and he notifies his buyer that this has been done. The finance house or bank in the importer's country is informed and its representative meets the importer and negotiates the terms of the credit he requires. If the importer is a distributor, the institution will arrange to offer medium-term credit to his retail buyers and will discuss with the distributor the short-term finance he needs. If he is a buyer, then a medium-term credit is arranged for him. The bank or finance house in Britain is notified when the credit is arranged and informs the exporter that this has been done and that he may proceed with the despatch of the goods. It collects payment from the union member in the importer's country and the exporter is paid in full in accordance with his normal terms of contract.

Where money is temporarily scarce, or rates of interest are high in the importer's country, it may be expedient for the financial institution in the exporter's country to lend the money, with perhaps the guarantee of the other union member. As far as the exporter is concerned, however, the effect is the same: he secures the necessary credit for his customer *without cost or recourse to himself.*

Examples of international credit unions are Export Finance International, European Credit Union and Eurocredit. These are associated with Forward Trust Ltd, Bowmaker Ltd and Lloyds and Scottish Finance Ltd, respectively which are hire-purchase finance houses owned by British banks. They are also all connected with continental financial institutions and Export Finance International also has correspondents in Australia and South Africa.

PROGRESS TEST 12

1. Summarise the ways in which the British Overseas Trade Board assists exporters. **(1)**
2. What is meant by factoring? **(2–4)**
3. Is factoring beneficial from the exporter's point of view? **(4)**
4. List the functions of a confirming house. **(5)**
5. What is an export house? **(6)**
6. How can exports be financed through a credit union? **(7)**

CHAPTER XIII

Export Credits Guarantee Department

FUNCTIONS OF ECGD

1. Insurance on a commercial basis. The Export Credits Guarantee Department is a government department established to provide insurance on a commercial basis for exporters. The Department is not meant to be an expense to the taxpayer because it must operate its business on solvent lines adopting normal insurance principles, with the exception of a small amount of business where, in the national interest and because of abnormal circumstances, insurance cover is given which is not on a commercial basis. Even in these cases, applications are most carefully vetted. In the early 1980s ECGD made substantial losses and had to make use of its reserves and raise its premiums in consequence.

Since 1930, when the credit insurance scheme commenced, the Department has insured an enormous volume of export business and the annual amount has increased rapidly to over £17,000 million in 1982–3 compared with £88 million in 1946–7. The proportion of total British exports insured with the Department has risen from 8 per cent in 1947 to around 35 per cent at the present time.

It is not the function of ECGD to provide finance for exports; it provides only insurance cover for exports. However, the fact that exports have been insured in this way gives an inducement to financial institutions, particularly the banks, to provide the necessary finance for exports in cases where they would otherwise not be willing to do so. Not only do ECGD guarantees help to bring forth finance for the exporter, but they may take the form of financial guarantees to banks and other financial institutions to cover loans direct to overseas buyers, to enable them to buy goods and services from Britain which they might otherwise be unable to finance.

The Export Credits Guarantee Department provides two types of insurance to exporters, comprehensive insurance and specific insurance. *Comprehensive* insurance is the term given to insurance of trade that is of a more or less repetitive nature, often with the same regular buyers and involving goods which are being sold for cash or on a short-term credit basis, and "extended" credit up to five years. *Specific* insurance is in respect of individual capital transactions overseas for expensive installations and construction projects, which are generally paid for on lengthy credit terms.

2. Advantages of ECGD cover.

(*a*) ECGD provides insurance against the political and economic risks, which include interference with the goods by a foreign government, cancellation of a valid import licence, inability to transfer exchange and war.

(*b*) The Department also provides insurance against the buyer's failure to pay. The creditworthiness of buyers can be quickly assessed by the Department, as it has a reference library of up-to-date information about the status of hundreds of thousands of buyers throughout the world.

(*c*) ECGD performs a function which is complementary to that of the banks, whose aim is necessarily to safeguard from loss, to the greatest possible extent, the finance which they make available for commercial ventures. This safeguard is provided by the Department's insurance cover and direct guarantees to the banks, which bring forth finance from the banks and other financial institutions which might not otherwise be provided.

(*d*) The climate of security fostered by ECGD enables exporters to offer better credit terms to buyers and to break into new markets.

3. The rates of premium.
Premium rates charged by the Department were greatly reduced as its business has expanded during the 1960s and 1970s but more recently it has been necessary for these to be increased to some extent. However, they are still quite low and are made up, as far as comprehensive cover is concerned, of a flat-rate premium payable at the beginning of each insurance year and a small payment per £100 in respect of goods insured in a particular month (*see* **9**).

On cover for specific capital goods exports, which is naturally more expensive, premiums have also been reduced as business has expanded. Even a contract with a buyer in one of the riskiest markets and involving payment over five years with a manufacturing period of one year would only cost about £4–£5 per £100.

4. National interest insurance.
In addition to the ordinary insurance business which accounts for the major part of its activities, ECGD is allowed to provide insurance cover up to certain limits to encourage exports to markets where prospects are too uncertain for normal cover on commercial lines to be given.

5. Revolving credit limits.
The assessment of the buyer's creditworthiness is one of the essential functions of underwriting the risks

involved in exporting. For large contracts the buyer is checked on each contract but, for consumer goods sold on terms of up to six months to a large number of buyers in a wide range of markets it is not necessary for each transaction to be referred to ECGD. The policy-holder may sell up to £250 of goods to a new buyer provided he has no adverse information on him and he can trade up to £5,000 with a buyer on whom he has obtained a satisfactory credit report. Beyond that the policy-holder is given a limit which is the maximum amount up to which he may trade with a particular buyer on short credit terms without referring to the Department. This allows the exporter maximum flexibility and freedom in the conduct of his day-to-day business. The figure allowed as a limit is *revolving*, i.e. as payments are made for past shipments, further shipments can be automatically covered within the terms of the policy. In practice, credit approvals run on year after year and are only reduced or cancelled if adverse information is received.

6. Percentage cover. ECGD does not provide 100 per cent cover against loss, as it is considered desirable that the exporter should carry a small percentage of any loss. This small amount acts as a discipline to ensure that:

(*a*) business is not entered into recklessly, without consideration of the financial consequences should the transaction fail to be carried through satisfactorily;

(*b*) buyers are not chosen indiscriminately;

(*c*) over-trading is discouraged;

(*d*) debtors will be pursued when the first signs of financial difficulty arise, thus helping to safeguard the insurer's position;

(*e*) the insured has an interest in maximising recoveries once a claim has been made. (Even after paying a claim, the Department does not normally interfere in the contract of sale between the exporter and the foreign buyer; as a result, for protection of its interests it must depend upon the exporter.)

Normally the percentage guaranteed by ECGD is 90 per cent for buyer risks and 90 or 95 per cent for political and economic risks; but in some markets where the economic and political prospects are especially hazardous the percentage cover may be lower.

7. Confidentiality. It is highly desirable that the importer should not become aware that the goods consigned to him are insured through ECGD, as this might encourage him to default. The Department therefore insists that its transactions must be treated as confidential, and only in exceptional circumstances will it agree to its interest being disclosed to the buyer.

COMPREHENSIVE GUARANTEES

8. The scope of comprehensive policies. Comprehensive short-term guarantees cover the export of consumer goods, durables and engineering manufactures sold on terms of payment normally to six months' credit, but terms can range over as much as five years.

The exporter takes out a policy under which he undertakes to insure the whole of his export turnover for a period of not less than a year. In some circumstances ECGD will accept business on a selected range of markets but for this business premiums are slightly higher.

9. The procedure. The exporter simply declares to ECGD once a month the total amount of business he has transacted under each policy. Individual contracts do not need to be referred to the Department (*see* 5 above).

The premiums on comprehensive short-term guarantees are paid in two ways. First, a non-refundable premium is paid at the commencement of each year of insurance based partly on the size of the policyholder's export turnover, partly on his claims record, and partly on the degree of use he makes of ECGD's credit limit service. All policyholders pay at least a minimum sum for each year of insurance. Second, a premium is payable on exports declared each month at the flat rate per £100 fixed at the commencement of each year of insurance. Policyholders who have pre-credit risk cover also pay the additional premium each month at a separate flat-rate.

10. The risks covered. Comprehensive policies cover the following types of risk:

(*a*) insolvency of the buyer;

(*b*) the buyer's failure to pay within six months of due date for goods which he has accepted;

(*c*) the buyer's failure to take up goods which have been despatched to him (where not caused or excused by the policy-holder's actions, and where ECGD decides that the institution or continuation of legal proceedings against the buyer would serve no useful purpose);

(*d*) a general moratorium on external debt decreed by the government of the buyer's country or of a third country through which payment must be made;

(*e*) any other action by the government of the buyer's country which prevents performance of the contract in whole or in part;

(*f*) political events, economic difficulties, legislative or administrative measures arising outside the UK which prevent or delay the transfer of payments or deposits made in respect of the contract;

(*g*) legal discharge of a debt (not being legal discharge under the proper law of the contract) in a foreign currency, which results in a shortfall at the date of transfer;

(*h*) war and certain other events preventing performance of the contract provided that the event is not one normally insured with commercial insurers;

(*i*) cancellation or non-renewal of a UK export licence or the prohibition or restriction on export of goods from the UK by law (this risk is covered only where the pre-credit risk section of the guarantee applies).

The proportion of any loss that will be paid by ECGD depends upon the cause of the loss. For insolvency of the buyer, or his failure to pay within six months (the first two of the risks listed above), the proportion covered is 90 per cent. For the other risks, apart from the buyer's failure to take up the goods, the proportion is 90 per cent if the cause arises before shipment and 95 per cent if it arises after shipment. Where the buyer fails to take up the goods the exporter must bear the "first loss" of 20 per cent of the full price and ECGD bears 90 per cent of the balance.

11. Payment of claims. The times of payment of claims under ECGD policies depend upon the cause of the loss as follows:

(*a*) *insolvency of the buyer*—immediately on proof of insolvency;

(*b*) *protracted default on goods accepted*—six months after due date of payment;

(*c*) *failure to take up goods*—one month after resale;

(*d*) *any other cause*—four months after due date of payment or date of the event causing the loss.

12. Supplemental extended terms guarantee. Where an exporter has a comprehensive policy for his short-term business he may take out a self-contained guarantee with its own operational and premium systems to cover credit in excess of six months. This *supplemental extended terms guarantee* covers goods, such as engineering goods, sold on credit terms of up to five years and, exceptionally, even longer. He must have an established pattern of continuing trade on these terms and may cover all markets or selected markets. Each proposed sale must be submitted to ECGD for approval as there is no discretionary limit.

13. Supplementary stocks guarantee. This supplemental policy is designed to cover the risks involved in holding stocks overseas in order to be able to undertake to provide delivery of spares and other goods. A limit is set for stocks in each market and a premium at a flat rate per £100 is paid at the outset on the aggregate of the stocks held.

14. External trade guarantee. If goods are shipped direct from one foreign country to another by a British merchant, he can obtain this type of guarantee to cover either all markets or a selected group of markets. It is limited to commodities or manufactures that do not compete with British products. The risks that can be covered by an *external trade guarantee* are restricted to 90 per cent of loss occurring through the insolvency of the buyer, or of loss occurring through war, revolution or civil disturbance, or through the failure or refusal of a government buyer to fulfil the terms of the contract.

15. Subsidiaries guarantee. A parent or associated company in the UK may obtain this type of guarantee to cover sales of goods by an overseas subsidiary. ECGD would normally insist upon covering the sale *to* the subsidiary before covering the sale *by* the subsidiary.

16. Bill guarantee. If an exporter has been insuring his goods under a comprehensive guarantee for some time and is transacting business by way of bills of exchange or promissory notes, he may obtain an ECGD *comprehensive bill guarantee*. This guarantee covers a credit period of 30 days to two years, and is an unconditional guarantee to the exporter's bank enabling the bank to make an advance to the exporter of 100 per cent against the presentation of the bill or promissory note and shipping documents up to an agreed revolving limit. The advance is made at $\frac{1}{8}$ per cent above base rate.

Until this bill has been accepted by the importer, the bank's advance is on a *with recourse* basis, but once the bill is accepted, or a promissory note issued by the importer, the bank's advance is converted into an outright purchase of the bill or promissory note on a *non-recourse* basis. The bank then relies solely on the bill guarantee. Upon default by the importer ECGD must reimburse the bank in full, but it has recourse to the exporter in respect of the difference between the amount it has to pay and the amount covered by the normal comprehensive policy.

The exporter pays a premium to ECGD of 25p per £100 each year on the revolving limit.

17. Open account guarantee. Exporters trading on cash against documents terms, or on an open account basis giving up to six months' credit, may obtain a *comprehensive open account guarantee* from ECGD. This is on rather similar lines to the bill guarantee. The bank advances up to 100 per cent of the net invoice amount of insured exports within a borrowing limit specified by ECGD and against each advance the exporter gives a promissory note to the bank with the appropriate repayment date (the last day of the month in which payment by the buyer is due). If the exporter fails to honour his promissory note ECGD pays the bank and in turn takes recourse to the exporter. As for bills guarantees, the banks charge interest at $\frac{5}{8}$ per cent above their base rate.

18. Comprehensive services guarantee. Earnings from invisible exports in the form of technical or professional services, copyright fees etc., can be covered by an ECGD *comprehensive services guarantee*. Where overseas services are performed on a recurrent basis, cover is obtainable on the same principle as comprehensive policies, with the policy-holder agreeing to insure the whole of his service's earnings and declaring his business as he does it. For other services, a *specific services guarantee* is issued, which covers all earnings under an individual services contract. The risks covered are insolvency of the buyer, protracted default in payment, delay in transfer of sterling, war and civil disturbances and any other cause of loss occurring outside the UK and beyond the control of buyer and seller. The proportion of loss covered on the first two risks is 90 per cent, both for the comprehensive and specific types of cover. For the other risks, the proportion is 95 per cent for the comprehensive cover and 90 per cent for the specific type.

SPECIFIC GUARANTEES

19. Capital goods transactions. Because transactions involving capital goods are usually large, the exporter cannot give ECGD the same spread of markets as can the exporter of consumer goods. Premiums cannot, therefore, be based on the spread of risks and must be the subject of negotiation between the exporter and the Department.

Cover is obtainable on a contracts or a shipments basis, but as lengthy manufacturing periods are usually involved, contracts policies are more common for capital projects.

20. The risks covered. The risks covered by specific policies are basically the same as those covered by the comprehensive policy but no cover is given against the failure of private buyers to take up exported goods. For sales of capital goods to government buyers ECGD will cover the risk of default by the buyer at any stage in the transaction. The top percentage of cover is 90 per cent, as against 95 per cent for comprehensive policies.

Sales on up to five years' credit are covered and the Department has in recent years been permitted to match terms of credit exceeding five years from shipment offered by foreign competitors with official credit insurance or equivalent support.

21. Negotiation of policies. When a contract for the supply of capital goods is being negotiated it is usual to start concurrent negotiations with ECGD about a specific policy. At this early stage, it is necessary to ascertain whether a policy would be obtainable for the country concerned and the probable cost of the cover. As the negotiations for the contract near completion, the Department will make a firm offer of cover which is normally valid for three months.

22. Aircraft policies. A modified form of specific policy is available to cover the sale of aircraft and aero-engines.

23. Constructional works policies. A *specific constructional works guarantee* can be obtained which covers both the supply of goods and the performance of services. This cover is given on an amount which includes price increases, provisional sums and interest, and which may also include a margin for the extra-contractual element in any arbitration award.

24. Assigning policies. ECGD policies are regarded as security in the normal banking sense. An exporter can assign to his bank his rights under all transactions covered by an ECGD policy. The Department gives formal acknowledgement of such an assignment, providing the bank with copies of relevant policy documents, such as credit limit approvals.

25. Bank guarantees. Where large-scale projects are concerned involving large amounts and credit terms of five years or more, it is usual for a bank to insist on a bank guarantee.

A *specific bank guarantee* is a supplement to the normal cover in which ECGD guarantees the exporter's bank direct that it will pay the bank unconditionally in the event of non-receipt of money due from the buyer. The bank is given complete security which is not conditional on the manner in which non-payment arises. Guarantees are available for individual contracts for the supply of capital goods on credit of not less than two years from shipment. They cover 100 per cent of loss through any default and payment is made three months after default. Contracts for an aggregation of small orders, or a bulk order of unit items from an overseas distributor, are not eligible. The banks charge a fixed rate of interest based on a scale of rates agreed at discussions between the major trading nations and revised from time to time. These "consensus" rates of interest at the time of writing range from 9.5 per cent in respect of loans for exports to relatively poor nations to 12.5 per cent where the sales are to the relatively rich nations.

Bank guarantees are operative from the date of acceptance of the goods or works by the buyer (or upon shipment of the goods where this takes place after acceptance).

When a bank guarantee is issued, the Department requires that the exporter must sign a separate recourse agreement to enable ECGD to recover from the exporter any payments made under the bank guarantee which it would not have made under the terms of the normal insurance policy.

BUYER CREDIT

26. Loans to overseas purchasers. The Export Credits Guarantee Department guarantees loans made by British and overseas banks direct to overseas purchasers to enable them to pay their suppliers on "cash" terms. These guarantees are called *buyer credit guarantees*.

Buyer credit guarantees are designed to assist the financing of capital projects for which normal supplier credit is inappropriate and are normally available only for projects costing £1 million or more.

The prospects of repayment must, of course, be satisfactory from the points of view both of the creditworthiness of the buyer and of the economic and political risks in the country concerned.

Buyer credit guarantees are confined to five years' credit except where it is established that longer terms are necessary to match foreign competition.

27. Procedure. Discussions with ECGD normally begin at an early stage, but not before the supplier is in negotiation with the buyer and has found a financial institution ready to finance the borrower in question.

The purchaser is normally required to pay 15–20 per cent of the contract price direct to the supplier out of his own resources, including an adequate down-payment on signature of the contract and a further instalment on or after ultimate commissioning of the plant. The remaining 80–85 per cent is paid to the supplier from the loan made to the buyer by the financial institution and guaranteed by ECGD as to 100 per cent of capital and interest against non-payment for any reason whatsoever.

Three legal agreements are involved:

    (*a*) a contract between the British supplier and the overseas buyer;
    (*b*) a loan agreement between a bank and an overseas borrower;
    (*c*) a financial agreement given by ECGD to the bank to cover the risk of non-payment of principal and interest.

28. Lines of credit. The system of buyer credit guarantees has been extended to provide cover for lines of credit to overseas governments and government agencies for farm mechanisation or electrification schemes or other large projects and in some cases for more general purposes. The governments or agencies do not have to commit themselves to any one supplier and, indeed, many suppliers are usually involved. Arrangements vary, but, typically, ECGD will give a guarantee to one bank which will have secured the backing of other banks and will undertake to provide credit up to a specified amount in respect of contracts for British goods or services falling within the terms of the credit agreement. Contract values may be as low as £10,000.

29. Investment insurance. To encourage British investment overseas ECGD offers a system of insurance for the potential risks involved. Insurance is available for investments of equity capital in the form of cash, plant or know-how, for loans to overseas enterprises and for certain guarantees of loans raised outside the UK. The investment must be new and the investor must apply for cover before becoming irrevocably committed to invest. The risks that are covered are expropriation, war damage and restrictions on remittances. The insurance covers 90 per cent of loss and ECGD's commitment is for fifteen years. An overall maximum insured amount is determined at the outset and within this limit the investor proposes a current insured amount at the beginning of each twelve months of the contract of insurance. A premium of 1 per cent is charged annually on the current insured amount and in addition $\frac{1}{2}$ per cent has to be paid on the difference between the current insured amount and the maximum insured amount.

PROGRESS TEST 13

1. Does ECGD provide finance for exports? **(1)**
2. What is the normal percentage cover (a) for buyer risks and (b) for political and economic risks? **(6)**
3. Explain the procedure when an exporter takes out a comprehensive ECGD policy. **(9)**
4. List the risks covered by an ECGD comprehensive policy. **(10)**
5. What is a supplemental extended terms guarantee? **(12)**
6. What is an external trade guarantee and in what circumstances can it be obtained? **(14)**
7. What is a bill guarantee? **(16)**
8. What is an open account guarantee? **(17)**
9. What is a specific ECGD guarantee? **(19–25)**
10. Comment on the purpose of an ECGD bank guarantee. **(25)**
11. What is an ECGD buyer credit guarantee? **(26–28)**
12. Describe the ECGD insurance cover available to overseas investors. **(29)**

CHAPTER XIV

International Monetary Relationships

EXCHANGE CONTROL

1. Purposes of control. Although exchange control in the UK was lifted in 1980 it still applies in some countries, and therefore British exporters must check the position very carefully before shipping goods abroad. The following comments are intended to give the reader an understanding of why and how exchange control is usually imposed.

In order to maintain the value of its currency in terms of other currencies, a country must endeavour to achieve a favourable balance of payments. If imports of goods and services from outside the monetary area exceed exports, the excess might have to be paid for from its stock of foreign currencies and claims upon foreign currencies. A country with an adverse balance of payments might therefore find it expedient to use exchange and trade controls in order to restrict imports. It will be appreciated that, even if the goods are to be paid for in the importer's currency, it might be converted into a foreign currency by the country receiving it, and therefore all imports are potentially a claim upon a country's stockpile of foreign currencies. Similarly, foreign investments must be limited because when capital is exported it has to be converted into a foreign currency.

To maximise a country's claims upon foreign currencies with which to build up a stockpile of them, exports must be encouraged, and it must be prepared to allow an inflow of foreign investment, although naturally it would not want too great a proportion of its industry to be owned by non-residents.

In wartime, control over trade and payments is obviously vital, for foreign trade is restricted. A country must import a large part of its requirements of foodstuffs and raw materials even in times of hostilities, yet exports are severely curtailed at such times. Import licensing is inevitable to ensure that only essential goods are brought into the country, and only where an import licence is given can the purchase of foreign currency be permitted. In wartime it may also be necessary for the state to take over private holdings of claims upon foreign currencies, i.e. holdings of foreign securities and property, and it is essential to ensure that all receipts of foreign currencies go into the central pool.

This involves a system whereby when goods are exported it is ensured that payment is made in the form most desirable for the nation, and that the proceeds are exchanged into the home currency by the recipient through an authorised dealer.

In peacetime exchange and trade control is obviously less necessary. In some countries it still exists, though in a much looser fashion, and this was the situation that prevailed in the UK until 1980 when it was abolished.

2. Trade control. A complete system of trade and exchange control includes tariffs and quotas. Tariffs are import duties imposed on goods coming into a country. Usually they are expressed as a percentage on the value of the goods but they can be expressed as an amount of the home currency per unit of commodity imported, e.g. 10p per 100 kg. Tariffs therefore make imports dearer and tend to discourage them but they do not prohibit the goods from being imported. They do not as a rule produce very much revenue to the country imposing them, being protective rather than revenue-earning. Tariffs may be imposed to protect a particular industry (especially an infant industry) from the effects of foreign competition, or they may be imposed in order to discourage imports in general.

Quotas are not revenue-earning at all, but are usually protective. A limit is set to the total quantity or value of a commodity which can be imported and import licences are issued until the quota is exhausted. The allocation of licences tends to be based upon the amount of the commodity imported by the applicant in some previous period, but this is not necessarily the basis.

3. The machinery used. It is normally a function of the central bank to be responsible for exchange control. The commercial banks act as agents for the central bank, requiring their customers to complete the necessary exchange control forms which are then submitted by the banks to the central bank. The commercial banks are allowed much discretion, in that they may approve applications themselves up to certain limits, and submit the forms after approval. In wartime these limits are much narrower than in peacetime, when only abnormal applications are submitted to the central bank for approval. In addition to the commercial banks, some other institutions are appointed to act as agents for the central bank, as gold and silver bullion dealers, for instance.

To ensure that exchange control regulations are enforced and not avoided, legal enactment is required and penalties are imposed when the law is broken.

4. Registration of foreign assets. To ensure that proceeds from the disposal of foreign securities and other assets are channelled into the official holdings of foreign currencies, the central bank requires holdings of such assets to be registered. It may also require that documents of title to the assets, such as share certificates, bonds and coupons, should be deposited with a bank, which alone can carry out transactions with them on behalf of its customer.

Securities owned by foreigners must also be registered, because if they are sold to a resident of the home country a claim on the home currency arises. Change of ownership must therefore be registered and it is usual to allow foreigners to sell securities only to one another so that no exchange problem occurs. This may be done by permitting the foreigner the sell the security for units of the home currency which must be put into a pool from which other foreigners must purchase the currency to buy securities. A pool of the home currency is thus created which is set aside for the financing of sales and purchases of securities by non-residents.

THE INTERNATIONAL MONETARY FUND

5. Aims of the Fund. The International Monetary Fund was established in 1946 as a result of the International Monetary Conference at Bretton Woods in the USA in 1944. At the conference it was decided to set up the Fund and also the International Bank for Reconstruction and Development (commonly known as the World Bank).

The objectives of the Fund are four-fold, as follows:

(*a*) to encourage international co-operation;
(*b*) to bring about an expansion of the economies of countries and an increase in international trade, with full employment;
(*c*) to achieve exchange stability;
(*d*) to remove trade restrictions and facilitate the settlement of international indebtedness.

Much of the very satisfactory degree of co-operation in international monetary affairs (such as the voluntary agreements by groups of countries to provide the UK with substantial amounts of credit to help her out of the sterling crises which have occurred from time to time) can be accredited to the existence of the Fund. Likewise, the Fund has been very successful in enabling countries to expand their economies and their foreign trade.

The IMF system of fixed exchange rates resulted in relative stability of exchange rates from 1946 to 1972, but since then the system has been abandoned and exchange rates allowed to float. There seems little likelihood of a restoration of the old system of fixed rates for many years to come, though in the EEC, under the European Monetary System (*see* **16**), exchange rates are now tied to one another.

6. Quotas and drawing rights. When a member country runs into balance of payments difficulties it can apply to the Fund for the loan of foreign currency or currencies with which to finance its deficit. For this purpose the IMF has a pool of gold and currencies contributed by its member countries on the basis of quotas allocated to them.

A country's ability to borrow from the IMF is determined by its quota. When applying to borrow, a country must show that it is taking appropriate action to put right its balance of payments deficit and to maintain the external value of its currency. Subject to this proviso, the Fund will lend up to a prescribed maximum.

7. International liquidity. The term *international liquidity* means the amount of gold and currencies and claims to gold and currencies which are available for use in the settlement of international indebtedness. This includes the gold and currency reserves of individual countries plus their potential IMF drawing rights. In addition, one must include loans from one country to another and such devices as the "swap agreement" whereby a country makes its currency available in exchange for that of another country.

A shortage of liquidity inhibits the growth of international trade because countries with inadequate access to gold and foreign exchange tend to restrict their imports for fear of incurring balance of payments deficits which they are unable to finance. It is for this reason that various measures have been taken from time to time to increase international liquidity. Several of these measures concern the International Monetary Fund.

On a number of occasions the Fund's quotas have been increased, which automatically increases the drawing rights of member countries, and in 1962 the *General Arrangements to Borrow* were agreed by ten member countries by which they undertook to lend some of their currencies to the IMF if asked to do so, in order to enable the Fund to lend them to other members. The Fund also has access to a pool of currencies made available to it by the oil-producing countries, which can be lent to oil-importing countries in addition to normal IMF drawing rights.

A further measure was the introduction of special drawing rights in 1970. These rights enable member countries to obtain finance from the Fund up to certain limits in addition to normal drawing rights, and not all of these drawings have to be repaid. The bulk of such drawings could therefore remain permanently outstanding and be included in the borrowing country's gold and convertible currency reserves.

8. A unit of account. Up to 1974 the IMF unit of account was the US dollar and in consequence any fluctuations in the value of the dollar affected the value of the Fund's assets. Since then the Fund has valued its assets in terms of SDRs (special drawing rights) the value of which is now related not only to the dollar but to a basket of five currencies. The weightings given to each of these currencies in revaluing the basket daily are based mainly on the exports of goods and services by the countries concerned but also take into account the fact that trade shares are not necessarily the sole determinant of a country's importance.

THE WORLD BANK AND ITS ANCILLARY INSTITUTIONS

9. Purpose of the Bank. The International Bank for Reconstruction and Development, commonly known as the World Bank, was set up in 1946, first to help finance the reconstruction of war-devastated countries, and then later to finance large capital projects which would quicken the rate of economic progress in the underdeveloped countries. The majority of loans so far made have gone to the Latin American states, to Africa and to Asia, for a multitude of projects such as the building of railways and docks, hydro-electric plants and irrigation schemes.

10. Sources of finance. The membership of the IBRD is similar to that of the IMF. Member countries subscribe capital to the Bank, the amount of which is based upon their importance in the world as measured by their national incomes and foreign trade. The chief source of finance, however, is by issuing bonds in the world's main financial markets and World Bank bonds have been issued in this way to obtain a variety of currencies.

As loans are repaid, so further loans can be made with the funds going back to the Bank. Furthermore, some of the Bank's loans have been sold, making funds available for new loans.

11. The procedure. Loans by the World Bank are made only to governments or to institutions with the backing of their governments. When requested to make a loan, the Bank sends a team of technical experts to the country concerned to advise on the project and to consider its suitability for the type of finance the Bank can provide. Loans are made on the basis of normal banking practice, which means that the projects must be economically justified and revenue-earning. The revenue (i.e. the improvement to the national income of the country concerned) must be sufficient to enable the loan to be repaid in the prescribed period.

Repayment of loans has to be made in the currency borrowed, and the period of the loan can be anything up to 30 years. The bank is therefore a source of long-term finance.

Loans are made at rates of interest which are roughly in line with market rates for the particular type of loan.

12. The International Finance Corporation. This offshoot of the World Bank was established in 1956 to meet two criticisms of the Bank, that it lent only to governments or government-sponsored institutions, and that it provided only safe loans. The IFC lends to institutions without government backing and is able to participate in equity capital, i.e. it is able to lend by buying ordinary shares in the institution carrying out the project.

The Corporation is open to members of the World Bank. The capital is very low, for the Corporation is designed to provide only relatively small loans, with the intention of encouraging private local investment in projects by the fact that the Corporation is interested in them.

Loans are for 5–15 years, and investments in share capital can be sold by the IFC when the time is ripe to do so. Interest is payable at market rates.

13. The International Development Association. The purpose of the Association, which was established in 1960, is to provide "soft" loans to underdeveloped countries. Loans may be for up to 50 years, repayable in the borrowing country's currency, and subject to a very low rate of interest or possibly no interest at all. The projects need not be revenue-earning.

This type of finance would obviously not be available from any firm or other business organisation, as it would not be a sound business proposition to lend on such terms. The Association is simply a way of channelling some of the aid to underdeveloped countries through a central institution.

SWAP AGREEMENTS

14. Mutual arrangements. Swap agreements are a device designed to increase international liquidity. They simply amount to arrangements whereby one central bank agrees to lend its currency to another central bank in exchange for a loan from that bank in its country's currency. For instance, the Federal Reserve Bank of New York might credit the account of the Bank of England with $100 million and in exchange the Bank of England would credit the account of the Federal Reserve Bank of New York the equivalent of $100 million in sterling. In this way, international liquidity is increased by $200 million, as the US can make use of $100 million of sterling and the UK can make use of $100 million of dollars.

15. "Stockpiling" currencies. On a number of occasions countries have agreed to hold surplus stocks of a currency which is weak and under pressure in order to help maintain and restore its exchange value. By "stockpiling" the currency in this way they keep it off the foreign exchange market until such time as the country of issue can buy it back directly from the central bank holding it, possibly borrowing on a longer-term basis from the International Monetary Fund in order to do so, or conceivably by borrowing Euro-currencies through the banking system.

EUROPEAN ECONOMIC COMMUNITY

16. The European Monetary System (EMS). This system came into operation in 1979 and its members are all the members of the European Economic Community with the exception of Britain and Greece. Member countries are required to keep the market rate for their currency within $2\frac{1}{4}$ per cent (6 per cent in the case of Italy) either side of an agreed central rate of exchange which is expressed in terms of the European Currency Unit (ECU). The value of the ECU is based on a weighted basket of member currencies. In order to maintain their currencies within the agreed margin member countries buy and sell their own currencies in the foreign exchange market but where there are excessive holdings of a particular currency these must be purchased by the country whose currency it is, using ECUs for the purpose.

A European Monetary Co-operation Fund has been established into which each member country has placed 20 per cent of its gold and currency reserves in exchange for the equivalent in ECUs.

The ultimate objective of the EMS is complete monetary union within the EEC but this is likely to take very many years to achieve.

PROGRESS TEST 14

1. Why does exchange control still exist in some countries? **(1)**
2. Distinguish between exchange control and trade control. **(2)**
3. What were the purposes of the establishment of the International Monetary Fund? **(5)**
4. What is meant by the term international liquidity and what steps have been taken in recent years to increase it? **(7)**
5. What is an SDR and how is its value measured? **(7, 8)**

6. Describe the International Bank for Reconstruction and Development and its functions.   (9, 10, 11)

7. How can central banks work together to support a currency that is weak?   (14, 15)

8. Explain the workings of the EMS.   (16)

The World Value of the Pound

The figures in Table XI are the rates of exchange for the pound against various currencies on 17th July 1984. In some cases, rates are nominal. Market rates are the average of buying and selling rates, except where they are shown to be selling rates only. In some cases, market rates have been calculated from the market rates of foreign currencies to which they are tied.

TABLE XI. THE WORLD VALUE OF THE POUND

Place and local unit		Value of £ sterling	Place and local unit		Value of £ sterling
Afghanistan	Afghani	99.00	Colombia	C. Peso	(F) 134.16
Albania	Lek	9.64	Comoro Islands	CFA Franc	574.5
Algeria	Dinar	(A) 6.57	Congo (Brazzaville)	CFA Franc	574.5
Andorra	{ French Franc	11.49	Costa Rica	Colon	(U) 57.95
	Spanish Peseta	212.4	Cuba	Cuban Peso	1.1415
Angola	Kwanza	(cm) 43.7625	Cyprus (S)	Cyprus £	0.7740
Antigua	E. Caribbean $	3.58			{ (cm) 9.30
Argentina	New Peso	73.035	Czechoslovakia	Koruna	{ n/c 16.18
Australia	Australian $	1.5825			{ 15.75 (6)
Austria	Schilling	26.275			{ 13.67
Azores	Portuguese Escudo	199.625			
			Denmark	Danish Krone	225 (sg)
Bahama (S)	Ba. Dollar	1.3260	Djibouti	Fr.	3.58
Bahrain (S)	Dinar	0.4970	Dominica (S)	E. Caribbean $	(o) 1.3260
Balearic Isles	Spa. Peseta	212.4	Dominican Repub.	Dominican Peso	(4) 3.978
Bangladesh (S)	Taka	33.16			
Barbados (S)	Barbados $	2.652	Ecuador	Sucre	{ (o) 85.29
Belgium	B. Franc	{ (cm) 75.725			{ (F) 117.79
		{ (fn) 76.70	Egypt	Egyptian £	{ (U) 1.0956
Belize	B. $	2.652			{ 1.5840 (5)
Benin	CFA Franc	574.5	Equatorial Guinea	Ekuele	424.8
Bermuda (S)	Bda. $	1.3260	Ethiopia	Ethiopian Birr	(P) 2.7000
Bhutan	Indian Rupee	14.99			
Bolivia	Bolivian Peso	(o) 2,652.0	Falkland Islands (S)	Falkland Is. £	1.0
Botswana (S)	Pula	1.76	Faroe Islands	Danish Krone	13.67
Brazil	Cruzeiro	2,388.26	Fiji Islands	Fiji $	1.4406
Brit. Virgin Isles	US $	1.3260	Finland	Markka	7.93845
Brunei (S)	Brunei $	2.8380	France	French Franc	11.49
Bulgaria	Lev	1.3846	French C'ty in Af.	CFA Franc	574.5
Burma	Kyat	11.3552	French Guiana	Local Franc	11.49
Burundi	Burundi Franc	160.16	French Pacific Is.	CFP Franc	202 (sg)
Cameroon Republic	CFA Franc	574.5	Gabon	CFA Franc	574.5
Canada	Canadian $	1.7585	Gambia (S)	Dalasi	5.00
Canary Islands	Spanish Peseta	212.4	Germany (East)	Ostmark	3.74
Cape Verde Isles	Cape V. Escudo	105.96	Germany (West)	Deutsche Mark	3.74
Cayman Islands (S)	Cay. Is. $	1.105	Ghana (S)	Cedi	46.1230
Cent. Af. Repub.	CFA Franc	574.5	Gibraltar (K)	Gibraltar £	1.0
Chad	CFA Franc	574.5	Greece	Drachma	147.56
Chile	C. Peso	121.03	Greenland	Danish Krone	13.67
China	Renminbi Yuan	2.9965	Grenada (S)	E. Caribbean $	3.58

121

Place and local unit		Value of £ sterling	Place and local unit		Value of £ sterling
Guadaloupe	Local Franc	11.49	Netherland Antilles	Antillian Guilder	2.3735
Guam	US $	1.3260	New Zealand (S)	NZ Dollar	N/A
Guatemala	Quetzal	1.3260	Nicaragua	Cordoba	13.235
Guinea Republic	Syli	32.05	Niger (Republic)	CFA Franc	574.5
Guinea Bissau	Peso	109.20	Nigeria (S)	Naira	1.061402 (sg)
Guyana (S)	Guyanese $	4.94	Norway	Norway Krone	10.825
Haiti	Gourde	6.63	Oman, Sul'ate of (S)	Rial Omani	0.4560
Honduras Repub.	Lempira	2.66			
Hong Kong (S)	HK $	10.31	Pakistan	Pakistan Rupee	18.53
Hungary	Forint	64.86†	Panama	Balboa	1.3260
			Papua N. Guinea (S)	Kina	1.1999
Iceland (S)	I. Krona	40.8150			317.64 (7)
India (S)	Ind. Rupee	14.99	Paraguay	Guarani	526.09 (8)
Indonesia	Rupiah	1,352.3			429.75 (9)
Iran	Rial	118.50 (sg)	Peru	Sol	exC (A) 4,557.27
Iraq	Iraq Dinar	0.4119	Philippines	Philippine Peso	23.30
Irish Republic (k)	Irish £	1.2205	Pitcairn Islands (S)	£ Sterling	—
Israel	Shekel	336.0		New Zealand £	N/A
Italy	Lira	2,300	Poland	Zloty	147.40
Ivory Coast	CFA Franc	574.5	Portugal	Portuguese Escudo	199.625
			Puerto Rico	US $	1.3260
Jamaica (S)	Jamaica Dollar	4.5565			
Japan	Yen	318.75	Qatar (S)	Qatari Ryal	4.8010
Jordan (S)	Jordan Dinar	0.505			
			Reunion, Ile de la	French Franc	11.49
Kampuchea	Riel	N/A	Romania	Leu	(cm) 6.53
Kenya (S)	Kenya Shilling	19.1750			(nc) 19.42
Kiribati	Australian $	1.5825	Rwanda	Rwanda Franc	136.53
Korea (Nth)	Won	1.6555‡			
Korea (Sth)	Won	1,067.28	St Christopher (S)	E. Caribbean $	3.58
Kuwait	Kuwait Dinar	0.3954	St Helena	St Helena £	1.0
			St Lucia	E. Caribbean $	3.58
Laos	New Kip	46.41	St Pierre	Local Franc	11.49
Lebanon	Lebanese £	7.7483	St Vincent (S)	E. Caribbean $	3.58
Lesotho	Maluti	1.9478	Salvador, El	Colon	3.3133
Liberia	Liberian $	1.3260	Samoa American	US $	1.3260
Libya	Libyan Dinar	0.3925	San Marino	Italian Lira	2,300
Liechtenstein	Swiss Franc	3.16	Sao Tome & Principe	Dobra	58.77
Luxembourg	Lux. Franc	75.725	Saudi Arabia	Saudi Ryal	4.64475
			Senegal	CFA Franc	574.5
Macao	Pataca	10.72	Seychelles	S. Rupee	9.18 (sg)
Madeira	Portuguese Escudo	199.625	Sierra Leone (S)	Leone	(o) 3.30
Malagasy Republic	MG Franc	707.50	Singapore (S)	Singapore $	2.8380
Malawi (S)	Kwacha	1.85	Solomon Islands (S)	Solomon Is. $	1.7195
Malaysia (S)	Ringgit	3.1040	Somali Republic	Somali Shilling	23.28
Maldive Islands (S)	Rufiyaa	10.01	South Africa (S)	Rand	1.9478
Mali Republic	Mali Franc	1.149	Spain	Peseta	212.4
	CFA Franc	574.5	Spanish ports in		
Malta (S)	Maltese £	0.6060	North Africa	Peseta	212.4
Martinique	Local Franc	11.49	Sri Lanka (S)	S.L. Rupee	33.29
Mauritania	Ouguiya	75.54	Sudan Republic	Sudan £ (U)	1.7445
Mauritius (S)	M. Rupee	18.0250	Surinam	S. Guilder	2.3735
Mexico	Mexican Peso	(F) 252.79	Swaziland (S)	Lilangeni	1.9478
		(C) 223.52	Sweden	S. Krona	10.95
Miquelon	Local Franc	11.49	Switzerland	Swiss Franc	3.16
Monaco	French Franc	11.49	Syria	Syria £	(A) (T) 10.0
Mongolia	Tugrik	4.75‡			(cm) 6.20
Montserrat	E. Caribbean $	3.58			
Morocco	Dirham	11.50 (sg)	Taiwan	New Taiwan $	52.29
Mozambique	Metical	(A) 56.26	Tanzania (S)	Tan. Shilling	22.7250
			Thailand	Baht	30.4250
Namibia	SA Rand	1.9478	Togo Republic	CFA Franc	574.5
Nauru	Australian Dollar	1.5825	Tonga Islands (S)	Pa'anga	1.5825*
Nepal	Nepalese Rupee	21.33	Trinidad (S)	Trinidad & Tob. $	3.1824
Netherlands	Guilder	4.22	Tunisia	Tunisian Dinar	0.9985 (sg)
			Turkey	Turkish Lira	488.44

Place and local unit		Value of £ sterling	Place and local unit		Value of £ sterling
Turks & Caicos	US $	1.3260	Vietnam	Dong	(o) 13.48
Tuvalu	Australian $	1.5825	Virgin Islands US	US Dollar	1.3260
Uganda (S)	Uganda Shilling	422.5	Western Samoa S.	Samoan Tala	(A) 2.31
United States	US Dollar	1.3260			
Uruguay	Uruguay Peso	72.62	Yemen (Nth)	Ryal	5.41 (sg)
Utd. Arab Emirates	UAE Dirham	4.856075	Yemen (Sth)	S. Yemen Dinar	(A) 0.4536
USSR	Rouble	1.0956	Yugoslavia	New Y. Dinar	189.7797
Upper Volta	CFA Franc	574.5			
			Zaire Republic	Zaire	48.0864
Vanuatu	Vatu	127.60	Zambia	Kwacha	2.35
Vatican	Italian Lira	2.300	Zimbabwe	Zimbabwe $	1.6630
Venezuela	Bolivar	(1) 5.69 (2) 9.92 (3) 17.07			

(A)	Approximate rate, no direct quotation available.		*	Rate is the transfer market (controlled).
(F)	Free rate.		†	Now one official rate.
(P)	Based on US dollar parities and going sterling/dollar rates.		‡	Based on gross rates against Russian rouble.
(S)	Member of the sterling area other than the scheduled territories.		(1)	Preferential rate for public sector debt and essential imports.
(T)	Tourist rate.		(2)	Preferential rate.
(U)	Unified rate. Applicable on all transactions except countries having a bilateral agreement with Egypt and who are not members of IMF.		(3)	Free rate for luxury imports, remittances of money abroad and foreign travel.
(Bas)	Basic rate.		(4)	Parallel rate.
(bg)	Buying rate.		(5)	Rate for remittances of foreign currency by Eyptians working abroad.
(Bk)	Bankers' rates.		(6)	Banknote rate.
(cm)	Commercial rate.		(7)	Rate for exports.
(ch)	Convertible rate.		(8)	Parallel rate.
(fn)	Financial rates		(9)	Rate for imports.
(exC)	Exchange certificate rate.			
(k)	Scheduled territory.			
(nc)	Non-commercial rate.			
(nom)	Nominal rate.			
(o)	Official rate.			
(sg)	Selling rate.			

Uniform Customs and Practice
for Documentary Credits
(1983 REVISION)

A.—GENERAL PROVISIONS AND DEFINITIONS

ARTICLE 1

These articles apply to all documentary credits, including, to the extent to which they may be applicable, standby letters of credit, and are binding on all parties thereto unless otherwise expressly agreed. They shall be incorporated into each documentary credit by wording in the credit indicating that such credit is issued subject to *Uniform Customs and Practice for Documentary Credits*, 1983 revision, ICC Publication No. 400.

ARTICLE 2

For the purposes of these articles, the expressions "documentary credit(s)" and "standby letter(s) of credit" used herein (hereinafter referred to as "credit(s)"), mean any arrangement, however named or described, whereby a bank (the issuing bank), acting at the request and on the instructions of a customer (the applicant for the credit),

(i) is to make a payment to or to the order of a third party (the beneficiary), or is to pay or accept bills of exchange (drafts) drawn by the beneficiary,
or

(ii) authorises another bank to effect such payment, or to pay, accept or negotiate such bills of exchange (drafts),
against stipulated documents, provided that the terms and conditions of the credit are complied with.

ARTICLE 3

Credits, by their nature, are separate transactions from the sales or other contract(s) on which they may be based and banks are in no way concerned with or bound by such contract(s), even if any reference whatsoever to such contract(s) is included in the credit.

ARTICLE 4

In credit operations all parties concerned deal in documents, and not in goods, services and/or other performances to which the documents may relate.

ARTICLE 5

Instructions for the issuance of credits, the credits themselves, instructions for any amendments thereto and the amendments themselves must be complete and precise.

In order to guard against confusion and misunderstanding, banks should discourage any attempt to include excessive detail in the credit or in any amendment thereto.

ARTICLE 6

A beneficiary can in no case avail himself of the contractual relationships existing between the banks or between the applicant for the credit and the issuing bank.

B.—FORM AND NOTIFICATION OF CREDITS

ARTICLE 7

(a) Credits may be either
  (i) revocable, or
  (ii) irrevocable.
(b) All credits, therefore, should clearly indicate whether they are revocable or irrevocable.
(c) In the absence of such indication the credit shall be deemed to be revocable.

ARTICLE 8

A credit may be advised to a beneficiary through another bank (the advising bank) without engagement on the part of the advising bank, but that bank shall take reasonable care to check the apparent authenticity of the credit which it advises.

ARTICLE 9

(a) A revocable credit may be amended or cancelled by the issuing bank at any moment and without prior notice to the beneficiary.
(b) However, the issuing bank is bound to:
  (i) reimburse a branch or bank with which a revocable credit has been made available for sight payment, acceptance or negotiation, for

any payment, acceptance or negotiation made by such branch or bank prior to receipt by it of notice of amendment or cancellation, against documents which appear on their face to be in accordance with the terms and conditions of the credit.

(*ii*) reimburse a branch or bank with which a revocable credit has been made available for deferred payment, if such branch or bank has, prior to receipt by it of notice of amendment or cancellation, taken up documents which appear on their face to be in accordance with the terms and conditions of the credit.

ARTICLE 10

(*a*) An irrevocable credit constitutes a definite undertaking of the issuing bank, provided that the stipulated documents are presented and that the terms and conditions of the credit are complied with:

(*i*) if the credit provides for sight payment—to pay, or that payment will be made;

(*ii*) if the credit provides for deferred payment—to pay, or that payment will be made, on the date(s) determinable in accordance with the stipulations of the credit;

(*iii*) if the credit provides for acceptance—to accept drafts drawn by the beneficiary if the credit stipulates that they are to be drawn on the issuing bank, or to be responsible for their acceptance and payment at maturity if the credit stipulates that they are to be drawn on the applicant for the credit or any other drawee stipulated in the credit;

(*iv*) if the credit provides for negotiation—to pay without recourse to drawers and/or bona fide holders, draft(s) drawn by the beneficiary, at sight or at a tenor, on the applicant for the credit or on any other drawee stipulated in the credit other than the issuing bank itself, or to provide for negotiation by another bank and to pay, as above, if such negotiation is not effected.

(*b*) When an issuing bank authorises or requests another bank to confirm its irrevocable credit and the latter has added its confirmation, such confirmation constitutes a definite undertaking of such bank (the confirming bank), in addition to that of the issuing bank, provided that the stipulated documents are presented and that the terms and conditions of the credit are complied with:

(*i*) if the credit provides for sight payment—to pay, or that payment will be made;

(*ii*) if the credit provides for deferred payment—to pay, or that payment will be made, on the date(s) determinable in accordance with the stipulations of the credit;

(*iii*) if the credit provides for acceptance – to accept drafts drawn by the beneficiary if the credit stipulates that they are to be drawn on the confirming bank, or to be responsible for their acceptance and payment at maturity if the credit stipulates that they are to be drawn on the applicant for the credit or any other drawee stipulated in the credit;

(*iv*) if the credit provides for negotiation—to negotiate without recourse to drawers and/or bona fide holders, draft(s) drawn by the beneficiary, at sight or at a tenor, on the issuing bank or on the applicant for the credit or on any other drawee stipulated in the credit other than the confirming bank itself.

(*c*) If a bank is authorised or requested by the issuing bank to add its confirmation to a credit but is not prepared to do so, it must so inform the issuing bank without delay. Unless the issuing bank specifies otherwise in its confirmation authorisation or request, the advising bank will advise the credit to the beneficiary without adding its confirmation.

(*d*) Such undertakings can neither be amended nor cancelled without the agreement of the issuing bank, the confirming bank (if any), and the beneficiary. Partial acceptance of amendments contained in one and the same advice of amendment is not effective without the agreement of all the above named parties.

ARTICLE 11

(*a*) All credits must clearly indicate whether they are available by sight payment, by deferred payment, by acceptance or by negotiation.

(*b*) All credits must nominate the bank (nominated bank) which is authorised to pay (paying bank), or to accept drafts (accepting bank), or to negotiate (negotiating bank), unless the credit allows negotiation by any bank (negotiating bank).

(*c*) Unless the nominated bank is the issuing bank or the confirming bank, its nomination by the issuing bank does not constitute any undertaking by the nominated bank to pay, to accept, or to negotiate.

(*d*) By nominating a bank other than itself, or by allowing for negotiation by any bank, or by authorising or requesting a bank to add its confirmation, the issuing bank authorises such bank to pay, accept or negotiate, as the case may be, against documents which appear on their face to be in accordance with the terms and conditions of the credit, and undertakes to reimburse such bank in accordance with the provisions of these articles.

ARTICLE 12

(*a*) When an issuing bank instructs a bank (advising bank) by any teletransmission to advise a credit or an amendment to a credit, and intends the mail confirmation to be the operative credit instrument, or the operative amendment, the teletransmission must state "full details to follow" (or words of similar effect), or that the mail confirmation will be the operative credit instrument or the operative amendment. The issuing bank must forward the operative credit instrument or the operative amendment to such advising bank without delay.

(b) The teletransmission will be deemed to be the operative credit instrument or the operative amendment, and no mail confirmation should be sent, unless the teletransmission states "full details to follow" (or words of similar effect), or states that the mail confirmation is to be the operative credit instrument or the operative amendment.

(c) A teletransmission intended by the issuing bank to be the operative credit instrument should clearly indicate that the credit is issued subject to *Uniform Customs and Practice for Documentary Credits*, 1983 revision, ICC Publication No. 400.

(d) If a bank uses the services of another bank or banks (the advising bank) to have the credit advised to the beneficiary, it must also use the services of the same bank(s) for advising any amendments.

(e) Banks shall be responsible for any consequences arising from their failure to follow the procedures set out in the preceding paragraphs.

ARTICLE 13

When a bank is instructed to issue, confirm or advise a credit similar in terms to one previously issued, confirmed or advised (similar credit) and the previous credit has been the subject of amendment(s), it shall be understood that the similar credit will not include any such amendment(s) unless the instructions specify clearly the amendment(s) which is/are to apply to the similar credit. Banks should discourage instructions to issue, confirm or advise a credit in this manner.

ARTICLE 14

If incomplete or unclear instructions are received to issue, confirm, advise or amend a credit, the bank requested to act on such instructions may give preliminary notification to the beneficiary for information only and without responsibility. The credit will be issued, confirmed, advised or amended only when the necessary information has been received and if the bank is then prepared to act on the instructions. Banks should provide the necessary information without delay.

C.—LIABILITIES AND RESPONSIBILITIES

ARTICLE 15

Banks must examine all documents with reasonable care to ascertain that they appear on their face to be in accordance with the terms and conditions of the credit. Documents which appear on their face to be inconsistent with one another will be considered as not appearing on their face to be in accordance with the terms and conditions of the credit.

ARTICLE 16

(a) If a bank so authorised effects payment, or incurs a deferred payment undertaking, or accepts, or negotiates against documents which appear on their face to be in accordance with the terms and conditions of a credit, the party giving such authority shall be bound to reimburse the bank which has effected payment, or incurred a deferred payment undertaking, or has accepted, or negotiated, and to take up the documents.

(b) If, upon receipt of the documents, the issuing bank considers that they appear on their face not to be in accordance with the terms and conditions of the credit, it must determine, on the basis of the documents alone, whether to take up such documents, or to refuse them and claim that they appear on their face not to be in accordance with the terms and conditions of the credit.

(c) The issuing bank shall have a reasonable time in which to examine the documents and to determine as above whether to take up or to refuse the documents.

(d) If the issuing bank decides to refuse the documents, it must give notice to that effect without delay by telecommunication or, if that is not possible, by other expeditious means, to the bank from which it received the documents (the remitting bank), or to the beneficiary, if it received the documents directly from him. Such notice must state the discrepancies in respect of which the issuing bank refuses the documents and must also state whether it is holding the documents at the disposal of, or is returning them to, the presentor (remitting bank or the beneficiary, as the case may be). The issuing bank shall then be entitled to claim from the remitting bank refund of any reimbursement which may have been made to that bank.

(e) If the issuing bank fails to act in accordance with the provisions of paragraphs (c) and (d) of this article and/or fails to hold the documents at the disposal of, or to return them to, the presentor, the issuing bank shall be precluded from claiming that the documents are not in accordance with the terms and conditions of the credit.

(f) If the remitting bank draws the attention of the issuing bank to any discrepancies in the documents or advises the issuing bank that it has paid, incurred a deferred payment undertaking, accepted or negotiated under reserve or against an indemnity in respect of such discrepancies, the issuing bank shall not be thereby relieved from any of its obligations under any provision of this article. Such reserve or indemnity concerns only the relations between the remitting bank and the party towards whom the reserve was made, or from whom, or on whose behalf, the indemnity was obtained.

ARTICLE 17

Banks assume no liability or responsibility for the form, sufficiency, accuracy, genuineness, falsification or legal effect of any documents, or for the general and/or particular conditions stipulated in the documents or superimposed thereon; nor do they assume any liability or responsibility for the description, quantity, weight, quality, condition, packing, delivery, value or existence of the goods represented by any documents, or for the good faith or acts and/or omissions, solvency, performance or standing of the consignor, the carriers, or the insurers of the goods, or any other person whomsoever.

ARTICLE 18

Banks assume no liability or responsibility for the consequences arising out of delay and/or loss in transit of any messages, letters or documents, or for delay, mutilation or other errors arising in the transmission of any telecommunication. Banks assume no liability or responsibility for errors in translation or interpretation of technical terms, and reserve the right to transmit credit terms without translating them.

ARTICLE 19

Banks assume no liability or responsibility for consequences arising out of the interruption of their business by Acts of God, riots, civil commotions, insurrections, wars or any other causes beyond their control, or by any strikes or lockouts. Unless specifically authorised, banks will not, upon resumption of their business, incur a deferred payment undertaking, or effect payment, acceptance or negotiation under credits which expired during such interruption of their business.

ARTICLE 20

(a) Banks utilising the services of another bank or other banks for the purpose of giving effect to the instructions of the applicant for the credit do so for the account and at the risk of such applicant.

(b) Banks assume no liability or responsibility should the instructions they transmit not be carried out, even if they have themselves taken the initiative in the choice of such other bank(s).

(c) The applicant for the credit shall be bound by and liable to indemnify the banks against all obligations and responsibilities imposed by foreign laws and usages.

ARTICLE 21

(*a*) If an issuing bank intends that the reimbursement to which a paying, accepting or negotiating bank is entitled shall be obtained by such bank claiming on another branch or office of the issuing bank or on a third bank (all hereinafter referred to as the reimbursing bank) it shall provide such reimbursing bank in good time with the proper instructions or authorisation to honour such reimbursement claims and without making it a condition that the bank entitled to claim reimbursement must certify compliance with the terms and conditions of the credit to the reimbursing bank.

(*b*) An issuing bank will not be relieved from any of its obligations to provide reimbursement itself if and when reimbursement is not effected by the reimbursing bank.

(*c*) The issuing bank will be responsible to the paying, accepting or negotiating bank for any loss of interest if reimbursement is not provided on first demand made to the reimbursing bank, or as otherwise specified in the credit, or mutually agreed, as the case may be.

D.—DOCUMENTS

ARTICLE 22

(*a*) All instructions for the issuance of credits and the credits themselves and, where applicable, all instructions for amendments thereto and the amendments themselves, must state precisely the document(s) against which payment, acceptance or negotiation is to be made.

(*b*) Terms such as "first class", "well known", "qualified", "independent", "official", and the like shall not be used to describe the issuers of any documents to be presented under a credit. If such terms are incorporated in the credit terms, banks will accept the relative documents as presented, provided that they appear on their face to be in accordance with the other terms and conditions of the credit.

(*c*) Unless otherwise stipulated in the credit, banks will accept as originals documents produced or appearing to have been produced:

(*i*) by reprographic systems;
(*ii*) by, or as the result of, automated or computerised systems;
(*iii*) as carbon copies,

if marked as originals, always provided that, where necessary, such documents appear to have been authenticated.

ARTICLE 23

When documents other than transport documents, insurance documents and commercial invoices are called for, the credit should stipulate by whom such documents are to be issued and their wording or data content. If the credit does not so stipulate, banks will accept such documents as presented, provided that their data content makes it possible to relate the goods and/or services referred to therein to those referred to in the commercial invoice(s) presented, or to those referred to in the credit if the credit does not stipulate presentation of a commercial invoice.

ARTICLE 24

Unless otherwise stipulated in the credit, banks will accept a document bearing a date of issuance prior to that of the credit, subject to such document being presented within the time limits set out in the credit and in these articles.

D1 Transport documents (documents indicating loading on board or dispatch or taking in charge)

ARTICLE 25

Unless a credit calling for a transport document stipulates as such document a marine bill of lading (ocean bill of lading or a bill of lading covering carriage by sea), or a post receipt or certificate of posting:

(a) banks will, unless otherwise stipulated in the credit, accept a transport document which:

(i) appears on its face to have been issued by a named carrier, or his agent, and

(ii) indicates dispatch or taking in charge of the goods, or loading on board, as the case may be, and

(iii) consists of the full set of originals issued to the consignor if issued in more than one original, and

(iv) meets all other stipulations of the credit.

(b) Subject to the above, and unless otherwise stipulated in the credit, banks will not reject a transport document which:

(i) bears a title such as "Combined transport bill of lading", "Combined transport document", "Combined transport bill of lading or port-to-port bill of lading", or a title or a combination of titles of similar intent and effect, and/or

(ii) indicates some or all of the conditions of carriage by reference to a source or document other than the transport document itself (short form/blank back transport document), and/or

(iii) indicates a place of taking in charge different from the port of loading and/or a place of final destination different from the port of discharge, and/or (*iv*) relates to cargoes such as those in Containers or on pallets, and the like, and/or

(*v*) contains the indication "intended", or similar qualification, in relation to the vessel or other means of transport, and/or the port of loading and/or the port of discharge.

(*c*) Unless otherwise stipulated in the credit in the case of carriage by sea or by more than one mode of transport but including carriage by sea, banks will reject a transport document which:

(*i*) indicates that it is subject to a charter party, and/or

(*ii*) indicates that the carrying vessel is propelled by sail only.

(*d*) Unless otherwise stipulated in the credit, banks will reject a transport document issued by a freight forwarder unless it is the FIATA Combined Transport Bill of Lading approved by the International Chamber of Commerce or otherwise indicates that it is issued by a freight forwarder acting as a carrier or agent of a named carrier.

ARTICLE 26

If a credit calling for a transport document stipulates as such document a marine bill of lading:

(*a*) banks will, unless otherwise stipulated in the credit, accept a document which:

(*i*) appears on its face to have been issued by a named carrier, or his agent, and

(*ii*) indicates that the goods have been loaded on board or shipped on a named vessel, and

(*iii*) consists of the full set of originals issued to the consignor if issued in more than one original, and

(*iv*) meets all the other stipulations of the credit.

(*b*) Subject to the above, and unless otherwise stipulated in the credit, banks will not reject a document which:

(*i*) bears a title such as "Combined transport bill of lading", "Combined transport document", "Combined transport bill of lading or port-to-port bill of lading", or a title or a combination of titles of similar intent and effect, and/or

(*ii*) indicates some or all of the conditions of carriage by reference to a source or document other than the transport document itself (short form/blank back transport document), and/or

(*iii*) indicates a place of taking in charge different from the port of loading, and/or a place of final destination different from the port of discharge, and/or (*iv*) relates to cargoes such as those in Containers or on pallets, and the like.

(*c*) Unless otherwise stipulated in the credit, banks will reject a document which:

(*i*) indicates that it is subject to a charter party, and/or

(*ii*) indicates that the carrying vessel is propelled by sail only, and/or

(*iii*) contains the indication "intended", or similar qualification in relation to

● the vessel and/or the port of loading—unless such document bears an on board notation in accordance with Article 27 (*b*) and also indicates the actual port of loading, and/or

● the port of discharge—unless the place of final destination indicated on the document is other than the port of discharge, and/or

(*iv*) is issued by a freight forwarder, unless it indicates that it is issued by such freight forwarder acting as a carrier, or as the agent of a named carrier.

ARTICLE 27

(*a*) Unless a credit specifically calls for an on board transport document, or unless inconsistent with other stipulation(s) in the credit, or with Article 26, banks will accept a transport document which indicates that the goods have been taken in charge or received for shipment.

(*b*) Loading on board or shipment on a vessel may be evidenced either by a transport document bearing wording indicating loading on board a named vessel or shipment on a named vessel, or, in the case of a transport document stating "received for shipment", by means of a notation of loading on board on the transport document signed or initialled and dated by the carrier or his agent, and the date of this notation shall be regarded as the date of loading on board the named vessel or shipment on the named vessel.

ARTICLE 28

(*a*) In the case of carriage by sea or by more than one mode of transport but including carriage by sea, banks will refuse a transport document stating that the goods are or will be loaded on deck, unless specifically authorised in the credit.

(*b*) Banks will not refuse a transport document which contains a provision that the goods may be carried on deck, provided it does not specifically state that they are or will be loaded on deck.

ARTICLE 29

(*a*) For the purpose of this article transhipment means a transfer and reloading during the course of carriage from the port of loading or place of dispatch or taking in charge to the port of discharge or place of destination either from one conveyance or vessel to another conveyance or vessel within the same mode of transport or from one mode of transport to another mode of transport.

(*b*) Unless transhipment is prohibited by the terms of the credit, banks will accept transport documents which indicate that the goods will be transhipped, provided the entire carriage is covered by one and the same transport document.

(*c*) Even if transhipment is prohibited by the terms of the credit, banks will accept transport documents which:

(*i*) incorporate printed clauses stating that the carrier has the right to tranship, or

(*ii*) state or indicate that transhipment will or may take place, when the credit stipulates a combined transport document, or indicates carriage from a place of taking in charge to a place of final destination by different modes of transport including carriage by sea, provided that the entire carriage is covered by one and the same transport document, or

(*iii*) state or indicate that the goods are in a Container(s), trailer(s), "LASH" barge(s), and the like and will be carried from the place of taking in charge to the place of final destination in the same Container(s), trailer(s), "LASH" barge(s), and the like under one and the same transport document.

(*iv*) state or indicate the place of receipt and/or of final destination as "CFS" (container freight station) or "CY" (container yard) at, or associated with, the port of loading and/or the port of destination.

ARTICLE 30

If the credit stipulates dispatch of goods by post and calls for a post receipt or certificate of posting, banks will accept such post receipt or certificate of posting if it appears to have been stamped or otherwise authenticated and dated in the place from which the credit stipulates the goods are to be dispatched.

ARTICLE 31

(*a*) Unless otherwise stipulated in the credit, or inconsistent with any of the documents presented under the credit, banks will accept transport documents stating that freight or transportation charges (hereinafter referred to as "freight") have still to be paid.

(*b*) If a credit stipulates that the transport document has to indicate that freight has been paid or prepaid, banks will accept a transport document on which words clearly indicating payment or prepayment of freight appear by stamp or otherwise, or on which payment of freight is indicated by other means.

(*c*) The words "freight prepayable" or "freight to be prepaid" or words of similar effect, if appearing on transport documents, will not be accepted as constituting evidence of the payment of freight.

(*d*) Banks will accept transport documents bearing reference by stamp or otherwise to costs additional to the freight charges, such as costs of, or disbursements incurred in connection with, loading, unloading or similar operations, unless the conditions of the credit specifically prohibit such reference.

ARTICLE 32

Unless otherwise stipulated in the credit, banks will accept transport documents which bear a clause on the face thereof such as "shippers load and count" or "said by shipper to contain" or words of similar effect.

ARTICLE 33

Unless otherwise stipulated in the credit, banks will accept transport documents indicating as the consignor of the goods a party other than the beneficiary of the credit.

ARTICLE 34

(*a*) A clean transport document is one which bears no superimposed clause or notation which expressly declares a defective condition of the goods and/or the packaging.

(*b*) Banks will refuse transport documents bearing such clauses or notations unless the credit expressly stipulates the clauses or notations which may be accepted.

(*c*) Banks will regard a requirement in a credit for a transport document to bear the clause "clean on board" as complied with if such transport document meets the requirements of this article and of Article 27(*b*).

D2 Insurance documents

ARTICLE 35

(*a*) Insurance documents must be as stipulated in the credit, and must be issued and/or signed by insurance companies or underwriters, or their agents.

(*b*) Cover notes issued by brokers will not be accepted, unless specifically authorised by the credit.

ARTICLE 36

Unless otherwise stipulated in the credit, or unless it appears from the insurance document(s) that the cover is effective at the latest from the date of loading on board or dispatch or taking in charge of the goods, banks will refuse insurance documents presented which bear a date later than the date of loading on board or dispatch or taking in charge of the goods as indicated by the transport document(s).

ARTICLE 37

(*a*) Unless otherwise stipulated in the credit, the insurance document must be expressed in the same currency as the credit.

(*b*) Unless otherwise stipulated in the credit, the minimum amount for which the insurance document must indicate the insurance cover to have been effected is the CIF (cost, insurance and freight ... "named port of destination") or CIP (freight/carriage and insurance paid to "named point of destination") value of the goods, as the case may be, plus 10 per cent. However, if banks cannot determine the CIF or CIP value, as the case may be, from the documents on their face, they will accept as such minimum amount the amount for which payment, acceptance or negotiation is requested under the credit, or the amount of the commercial invoice, whichever is the greater.

ARTICLE 38

(*a*) Credits should stipulate the type of insurance required and, if any, the additional risks which are to be covered. Imprecise terms such as "usual risks" or "customary risks" should not be used; if they are used, banks will accept insurance documents as presented, without responsibility for any risks not being covered.

(*b*) Failing specific stipulations in the credit, banks will accept insurance documents as presented, without responsibility for any risks not being covered.

ARTICLE 39

Where a credit stipulates "insurance against all risks", banks will accept an insurance document which contains any "all risks" notation or clause, whether or not bearing the heading "all risks", even if indicating that certain risks are excluded, without responsibility for any risk(s) not being covered.

ARTICLE 40

Banks will accept an insurance document which indicates that the cover is subject to a franchise or an excess (deductible), unless it is specifically stipulated in the credit that the insurance must be issued irrespective of percentage.

D3 Commercial invoice

ARTICLE 41

(*a*) Unless otherwise stipulated in the credit, commercial invoices must be made out in the name of the applicant for the credit.

(*b*) Unless otherwise stipulated in the credit, banks may refuse commercial invoices issued for amounts in excess of the amount permitted by the credit. Nevertheless, if a bank authorised to pay, incur a deferred payment undertaking, accept, or negotiate under a credit accepts such invoices, its decision will be binding upon all parties, provided such bank has not paid, incurred a deferred payment undertaking, accepted or effected negotiation for an amount in excess of that permitted by the credit.

(*c*) The description of the goods in the commercial invoice must correspond with the description in the credit. In all other documents, the goods may be described in general terms not inconsistent with the description of the goods in the credit.

D4 Other documents

ARTICLE 42

If a credit calls for an attestation or certification of weight in the case of transport other than by sea, banks will accept a weight stamp or declaration of weight which appears to have been superimposed on the transport document by the carrier or his agent unless the credit specifically stipulates that the attestation or certification of weight must be by means of a separate document.

E.—MISCELLANEOUS PROVISIONS

Quantity and amount

ARTICLE 43

(*a*) The words "about", "circa" or similar expressions used in connection with the amount of the credit or the quantity or the unit price stated in the credit are to be construed as allowing a difference not to exceed 10 per cent more or 10 per cent less than the amount or the quantity or the unit price to which they refer.

(b) Unless a credit stipulates that the quantity of the goods specified must not be exceeded or reduced, a tolerance of 5 per cent more or 5 per cent less will be permissible, even if partial shipments are not permitted, always provided that the amount of the drawings does not exceed the amount of the credit. This tolerance does not apply when the credit stipulates the quantity in terms of a stated number of packing units or individual items.

Partial drawings and/or shipments

ARTICLE 44

(a) Partial drawings and/or shipments are allowed, unless the credit stipulates otherwise.

(b) Shipments by sea, or by more than one mode of transport but including carriage by sea, made on the same vessel and for the same voyage, will not be regarded as partial shipments, even if the transport documents indicating loading on board bear different dates of issuance and/or indicate different ports of loading on board.

(c) Shipments made by post will not be regarded as partial shipments if the post receipts or certificates of posting appear to have been stamped or otherwise authenticated in the place from which the credit stipulates the goods are to be dispatched, and on the same date.

(d) Shipments made by modes of transport other than those referred to in paragraphs (b) and (c) of this article will not be regarded as partial shipments, provided the transport documents are issued by one and the same carrier or his agent and indicate the same date of issuance, the same place of dispatch or taking in charge of the goods, and the same destination.

Drawings and/or shipments by instalments

ARTICLE 45

If drawings and/or shipments by instalments within given periods are stipulated in the credit and any instalment is not drawn and/or shipped within the period allowed for that instalment, the credit ceases to be available for that and any subsequent instalments, unless otherwise stipulated in the credit.

Expiry date and presentation

ARTICLE 46

(a) All credits must stipulate an expiry date for presentation of documents for payment, acceptance or negotiation.

(*b*) Except as provided in Article 48(*a*), documents must be presented on or before such expiry date.

(*c*) If an issuing bank states that the credit is to be available "for one month", "for six months" or the like, but does not specify the date from which the time is to run, the date of issuance of the credit by the issuing bank will be deemed to be the first day from which such time is to run. Banks should discourage indication of the expiry date of the credit in this manner.

ARTICLE 47

(*a*) In addition to stipulating an expiry date for presentation of documents, every credit which calls for a transport document(s) should also stipulate a specified period of time after the date of issuance of the transport document(s) during which presentation of documents for payment, acceptance or negotiation must be made. If no such period of time is stipulated, banks will refuse documents presented to them later than 21 days after the date of issuance of the transport document(s). In every case, however, documents must be presented not later than the expiry date of the credit.

(*b*) For the purpose of these articles, the date of issuance of a transport document(s) will be deemed to be:

(*i*) in the case of a transport document evidencing dispatch, or taking in charge, or receipt of goods for shipment by a mode of transport other than by air—the date of issuance indicated on the transport document or the date of the reception stamp thereon whichever is the later.

(*ii*) in the case of a transport document evidencing carriage by air—the date of issuance indicated on the transport document or, if the credit stipulates that the transport document shall indicate an actual flight date, the actual flight date as indicated on the transport document.

(*iii*) in the case of a transport document evidencing loading on board a named vessel—the date of issuance of the transport document or, in the case of an on board notation in accordance with Article 27(*b*), the date of such notation.

(*iv*) in cases to which Article 44(*b*) applies, the date determined as above of the latest transport document issued.

ARTICLE 48

(*a*) If the expiry date of the credit and/or the last day of the period of time after the date of issuance of the transport document(s) for presentation of documents stipulated by the credit or applicable by virtue of Article 47 falls on a day on which the bank to which presentation has to be made is closed for reasons other than those referred to in Article 19, the stipulated expiry date and/or the last day of the period of time after the date of issuance of the transport document(s) for presentation of documents, as the case may be, shall be extended to the first following business day on which such bank is open.

(*b*) The latest date for loading on board, or dispatch, or taking in charge shall not be extended by reason of the extension of the expiry date and/or the period of time after the date of issuance of the transport document(s) for presentation of document(s) in accordance with this article. If no such latest date for shipment is stipulated in the credit or amendments thereto, banks will reject transport documents indicating a date of issuance later than the expiry date stipulated in the credit or amendments thereto.

(*c*) The bank to which presentation is made on such first following business day must add to the documents its certificate that the documents were presented within the time limits extended in accordance with Article 48(*a*) of the *Uniform Customs and Practice for Documentary Credits*, 1983 revision, ICC Publication No. 400.

ARTICLE 49

Banks are under no obligation to accept presentation of documents outside the banking hours.

Loading on board, dispatch and taking in charge (shipment)

ARTICLE 50

(*a*) Unless otherwise stipulated in the credit, the expression "shipment" used in stipulating an earliest and/or a latest shipment date will be understood to include the expressions "loading on board", "dispatch" and "taking in charge".

(*b*) The date of issuance of the transport document determined in accordance with Article 47(*b*) will be taken to be the date of shipment.

(*c*) Expressions such as "prompt", "immediately", "as soon as possible", and the like should not be used. If they are used, banks will interpret them as a stipulation that shipment is to be made within thirty days from the date of issuance of the credit by the issuing bank.

(*d*) If the expression "on or about" and similar expressions are used, banks will interpret them as a stipulation that shipment is to be made during the period from five days before to five days after the specified date, both end days included.

Date terms

ARTICLE 51

The words "to", "until", "till", "from", and words of similar import applying to any date term in the credit will be understood to include the date mentioned. The word "after" will be understood to exclude the date mentioned.

ARTICLE 52

The terms "first half", "second half" of a month shall be construed respectively as from the 1st to the 15th, and the 16th to the last day of each month, inclusive.

ARTICLE 53

The terms "beginning", "middle", or "end" of a month shall be construed respectively as from the 1st to the 10th, the 11th to the 20th, and the 21st to the last day of each month, inclusive.

F.—TRANSFER

ARTICLE 54

(a) A transferable credit is a credit under which the beneficiary has the right to request the bank called upon to effect payment or acceptance or any bank entitled to effect negotiation to make the credit available in whole or in part to one or more other parties (second beneficiaries).

(b) A credit can be transferred only if it is expressly designated as "transferable" by the issuing bank. Terms such as "divisible", "fractionable", "assignable", and "transmissible" add nothing to the meaning of the term "transferable" and shall not be used.

(c) The bank requested to effect the transfer (transferring bank), whether it has confirmed the credit or not, shall be under no obligation to effect such transfer except to the extent and in the manner expressly consented to by such bank.

(d) Bank charges in respect of transfers are payable by the first beneficiary unless otherwise specified. The transferring bank shall be under no obligation to effect the transfer until such charges are paid.

(e) A transferable credit can be transferred once only. Fractions of a transferable credit (not exceeding in the aggregate the amount of the credit) can be transferred separately, provided partial shipments are not prohibited, and the aggregate of such transfers will be considered as constituting only one transfer of the credit. The credit can be transferred only on the terms and conditions specified in the original credit, with the exception of the amount of the credit, of any unit prices stated therein, of the period of validity, of the last date for presentation of documents in accordance with Article 47 and the period for shipment, any or all of which may be reduced or curtailed, or the percentage for which insurance cover must be effected, which may be increased in such a way as to provide the amount of cover stipulated in the original credit, or these articles. Additionally, the name of the first beneficiary can be substituted for that of the applicant for the credit, but if the name of the applicant for the credit is specifically required by the original credit to appear in any document other than the invoice, such requirement must be fulfilled.

(f) The first beneficiary has the right to substitute his own invoices (and drafts if the credit stipulates that drafts are to be drawn on the applicant for the credit) in exchange for those of the second beneficiary, for amounts not in excess of the original amount stipulated in the credit and for the original unit prices if stipulated in the credit, and upon such substitution of invoices (and drafts) the first beneficiary can draw under the credit for the difference, if any, between his invoices and the second beneficiary's invoices. When a credit has been transferred and the first beneficiary is to supply his own invoices (and drafts) in exchange for the second beneficiary's invoices (and drafts) but fails to do so on first demand, the paying, accepting or negotiating bank has the right to deliver to the issuing bank the documents received under the credit, including the second beneficiary's invoices (and drafts) without further responsibility to the first beneficiary.

(g) Unless otherwise stipulated in the credit, the first beneficiary of a transferable credit may request that the credit be transferred to a second beneficiary in the same country, or in another country. Further, unless otherwise stipulated in the credit, the first beneficiary shall have the right to request that payment or negotiation be effected to the second beneficiary at the place to which the credit has been transferred, up to and including the expiry date of the original credit, and without prejudice to the first beneficiary's right subsequently to substitute his own invoices and drafts (if any) for those of the second beneficiary and to claim any difference due to him.

Assignment of proceeds

ARTICLE 55

The fact that a credit is not stated to be transferable shall not affect the beneficiary's right to assign any proceeds to which he may be, or may become, entitled under such credit, in accordance with the provisions of the applicable law.

The *Uniform Customs and Practice for Documentary Credits* were proposed by the ICC Commission on Banking Technique and Practice.

This Commission brings together bankers from throughout the world with the object of:

● defining, simplifying and harmonising the practices and terminology used in international banking;
● expressing the views of bankers before relevant international organisations, in particular the United Nations Commission on International Trade Law (UNCITRAL);
● serving as a forum for bankers to discuss common problems.

Each ICC National Committee may appoint members of the Banking Commission, and of the twenty other ICC Commissions covering most subject areas of interest to international business.

Uniform Rules for Collections

GENERAL PROVISIONS AND DEFINITIONS

(A) The provisions and definitions and the following articles apply to all collections as defined in (B) below and are binding upon all parties thereto unless otherwise expressly agreed or unless contrary to the provisions of a national, state or local law and/or regulation which cannot be departed from.

(B) For the purpose of such provisions, definitions and articles:

1. (*i*) "Collection" means the handling by banks, on instructions received, of documents as defined in (*ii*) below, in order to

   (*a*) obtain acceptance and/or, as the case may be, payment, or
   (*b*) deliver commercial documents against acceptance and/or, as the case may be, against payment, or
   (*c*) deliver documents on other terms and conditions.

(*ii*) "Documents" means financial documents and/or commercial documents

   (*a*) "financial documents" means bills of exchange, promissory notes, cheques, payment receipts or other similar instruments used for obtaining the payment of money;
   (*b*) "commercial documents" means invoices, shipping documents, documents of title or other similar documents, or any other documents whatsoever, not being financial documents.

(*iii*) "Clean collection" means collection of financial documents not accompanied by commercial documents.

(*iv*) "Documentary collection" means collection of

   (*a*) financial documents accompanied by commercial documents;
   (*b*) commercial documents not accompanied by financial documents.

2. The "parties thereto" are:

   (*i*) the "principal" who is the customer entrusting the operation of collection to his bank;

(*ii*) the "remitting bank" which is the bank to which the principal has entrusted the operation of collection;

(*iii*) the "collecting bank" which is any bank, other than the remitting bank, involved in processing the collection order;

(*iv*) the "presenting bank" which is the collecting bank making presentation to the drawee.

3. The "drawee" is the one to whom presentation is to be made according to the collection order.

(C) All documents sent for collection must be accompanied by a collection order giving complete and precise instructions. Banks are only permitted to act upon the instructions given in such collection order, and in accordance with these rules.

If any bank cannot, for any reason, comply with the instructions given in the collection order received by it, it must immediately advise the party from whom it received the collection order.

LIABILITIES AND RESPONSIBILITIES

ARTICLE 1

Banks will act in good faith and exercise reasonable care.

ARTICLE 2

Banks must verify that the documents received appear to be as listed in the collection order and must immediately advise the party from whom the collection order was received of any documents missing.

Banks have no further obligation to examine the documents.

ARTICLE 3

For the purpose of giving effect to the instructions of the principal, the remitting bank will utilise as the collecting bank:

(*i*) the collecting bank nominated by the principal, or, in the absence of such nomination,

(*ii*) any bank, of its own or another bank's choice, in the country of payment or acceptance, as the case may be.

The documents and the collection order may be sent to the collecting bank directly or through another bank as intermediary.

Banks utilising the services of other banks for the purpose of giving effect to the instructions of the principal do so for the account of and at the risk of the latter.

The principal shall be bound by and liable to indemnify the banks against all obligations and responsibilities imposed by foreign laws or usages.

ARTICLE 4

Banks concerned with a collection assume no liability or responsibility for the consequences arising out of delay and/or loss in transit of any messages, letters or documents, or for delay, mutilation or other errors arising in the transmission of cables, telegrams, telex or communication by electronic systems, or for errors in translation or interpretation of technical terms.

ARTICLE 5

Banks concerned with a collection assume no liability or responsibility for the consequences arising out of delay and/or loss in transit of any Acts of God, riots, civil commotions, insurrections, wars, or any other causes beyond their control or by any strikes or lockouts.

ARTICLE 6

Goods should not be despatched direct to the address of a bank or consigned to a bank without prior agreement on the part of that bank.

In the event of goods being despatched direct to the address of a bank or consigned to a bank for delivery to a drawee against payment or acceptance or upon other terms without prior agreement on the part of that bank, the bank has no obligation to take delivery of the goods, which remain at the risk and responsibility of the party despatching the goods.

PRESENTATION

ARTICLE 7

Documents are to be presented to the drawee in the form in which they are received, except that remitting and collecting banks are authorised to affix any necessary stamps, at the expense of the principal unless otherwise instructed, and to make any necessary endorsements or place any rubber stamps or other identifying marks or symbols customary to or required for the collection operation.

ARTICLE 8

Collection orders should bear the complete address of the drawee or of the domicile at which presentation is to be made. If the address is incomplete or incorrect, the collecting bank may, without obligation and responsibility on its part, endeavour to ascertain the proper address.

ARTICLE 9

In the case of documents payable at sight the presenting bank must make presentation for payment without delay.

In the case of documents payable at a tenor other than sight the presenting bank must, where acceptance is called for, make presentation for acceptance without delay, and where payment is called for, make presentation for payment not later than the appropriate maturity date.

ARTICLE 10

In respect of a documentary collection including a bill of exchange payable at a future date, the collection order should state whether the commercial documents are to be released to the drawee against acceptance (D/A) or against payment (D/P).

In the absence of such statement, the commercial documents will be released only against payment.

PAYMENT

ARTICLE 11

In the case of documents payable in the currency of the country of payment (local currency), the presenting bank must, unless otherwise instructed in the collection order, only release the documents to the drawee against payment in local currency which is immediately available for disposal in the manner specified in the collection order.

ARTICLE 12

In the case of documents payable in a currency other than that of the country of payment (foreign currency) the presenting bank must, unless otherwise instructed in the collection order, only release the documents to the drawee against payment in the relative foreign currency which can immediately be remitted in accordance with the instructions given in the collection order.

ARTICLE 13

In respect of clean collections partial payments may be accepted if and to the extent to which and on the conditions on which partial payments are authorised by the law in force in the place of payment. The documents will only be released to the drawee when full payment thereof has been received.

In respect of documentary collections partial payments will only be accepted if specifically authorised in the collection order. However, unless otherwise instructed, the presenting bank will only release the documents to the drawee after full payment has been received.

In all cases partial payments will only be accepted subject to compliance with the provisions of either Article 11 or Article 12 as appropriate. Partial payment, if accepted, will be dealt with in accordance with the provisions of Article 14.

ARTICLE 14

Amounts collected (less charges and/or disbursements and/or expenses where applicable) must be made available without delay to the bank from which the collection order was received in accordance with the instructions contained in the collection order.

ACCEPTANCE

ARTICLE 15

The presenting bank is responsible for seeing that the form of the acceptance of a bill of exchange appears to be complete and correct, but is not responsible for the genuineness of any signature or for the authority of any signatory to sign the acceptance.

PROMISSORY NOTES, RECEIPTS AND OTHER SIMILAR INSTRUMENTS

ARTICLE 16

The presenting bank is not responsible for the genuineness of any signature or for the authority of any signatory to sign a promissory note, receipt, or other similar instrument.

PROTEST

ARTICLE 17

The collection order should give specific instructions regarding protest (or other legal process in lieu thereof), in the event of non-acceptance or non-payment.

In the absence of such specific instructions the banks concerned with the collection have no obligation to have the documents protested (or subjected to other legal process in lieu thereof) for non-payment or non-acceptance.

Any charges and/or expenses incurred by banks in connection with such protest or other legal process will be for the account of the principal.

CASE-OF-NEED (PRINCIPAL'S REPRESENTATIVE) AND PROTECTION OF GOODS

ARTICLE 18

If the principal nominates a representative to act as case-of-need in the event of non-acceptance and/or non-payment the collection order should clearly and fully indicate the powers of such case-of-need.

In the absence of such indication banks will not accept any instructions from the case-of-need.

ARTICLE 19

Banks have no obligation to take any action in respect of the goods to which a documentary collection relates.

Nevertheless in the case that banks take action for the protection of the goods, whether instructed or not, they assume no liability or responsibility with regard to the fate and/or condition of the goods and/or for any acts and/or omissions on the part of any third parties entrusted with the custody and/or protection of the goods. However, the collecting bank must immediately advise the bank from which the collection order was received of any such action taken.

Any charges and/or expenses incurred by banks in connection with any action for the protection of the goods will be for the account of the principal.

ADVICE OF FATE, ETC.

ARTICLE 20

Collecting banks are to advise fate in accordance with the following rules:

(*i*) Form of advice—All advices or information from the collecting bank to the bank from which the collection order was received, must bear appropriate detail including, in all cases, the latter bank's reference number of the collection order.

(*ii*) Method of advice—In the absence of specific instructions the collecting bank must send all advices to the bank from which the collection order was received by quickest mail but, if the collecting bank considers the matter to be urgent, quicker methods such as cable, telegram, telex, or communication by electronic systems, etc. may be used at the expense of the principal.

(*iii*) (*a*) Advice of payment—The collecting bank must send without delay advice of payment to the bank from which the collection order was received, detailing the amount or amounts collected, charges and/or disbursements and/or expenses deducted, where appropriate, and method of disposal of the funds.

(*b*) Advice of acceptance—The collecting bank must send without delay advice of acceptance to the bank from which the collection order was received.

(*c*) Advice of non-payment or non-acceptance—The collecting bank must send without delay advice of non-payment or advice of non-acceptance to the bank from which the collection order was received.

The presenting bank should endeavour to ascertain the reasons for such non-payment or non-acceptance and advise accordingly the bank from which the collection order was received.

On receipt of such advice the remitting bank must, within a reasonable time, give appropriate instructions as to the further handling of the documents. If such instructions are not received by the presenting bank within 90 days from its advice of non-payment or non-acceptance, the documents may be returned to the bank from which the collection order was received.

INTEREST, CHARGES AND EXPENSES

ARTICLE 21

If the collection order includes an instruction to collect interest which is not embodied in the accompanying financial document(s), if any, and the drawee refuses to pay such interest, the presenting bank may deliver the document(s) against payment or acceptance as the case may be without collecting such interest, unless the collection order expressly states that such interest may not be waived. Where such interest is to be collected the collection order must bear an indication of the rate of interest and the period covered. When payment of interest has been refused the presenting bank must inform the bank from which the collection order was received accordingly.

If the documents include a financial document containing an unconditional and definitive interest clause the interest amount is deemed to form part of the amount of the documents to be collected. Accordingly, the interest amount is payable in addition to the principal amount shown in the financial document and may not be waived unless the collection order so authorises.

If the collection order includes an instruction that collection charges and/or expenses are to be for account of the drawee and the drawee refuses to pay them, the presenting bank may deliver the document(s) against payment or acceptance as the case may be without collecting charges and/or expenses unless the collection order expressly states that such charges and/or expenses may not be waived. When payment of collection charges and/or expenses has been refused the presenting bank must inform the bank from which the collection order was received accordingly. Whenever collection charges and/or expenses are so waived they will be for the account of the principal, and may be deducted from the proceeds.

Should a collection order specifically prohibit the waiving of collection charges and/or expenses then neither the remitting nor collecting nor presenting bank shall be responsible for any costs or delays resulting from this prohibition.

In all cases where in the express terms of a collection order, or under these Rules, disbursements and/or expenses and/or collection charges are to be borne by the principal, the collecting bank(s) shall be entitled promptly to recover outlays in respect of disbursements and expenses and charges from the bank from which the collection order was received and the remitting bank shall have the right promptly to recover from the principal any amount so paid out by it, together with its own disbursements, expenses and charges, regardless of the fate of the collection.

Examination Technique

Questions in Finance of Foreign Trade fall into two distinct categories: (1) *essay* questions, requiring the candidate to define terms used in the questions and to analyse and discuss problems, e.g. "What is a documentary credit and how can an importer protect himself from the fact that persons handling the credit are dealing with documents and not goods?" (2) *arithmetical* questions, requiring the candidate to calculate the cost of or the proceeds of particular foreign exchange transactions.

1. Essay questions. The following general points should always be borne in mind in answering questions that involve writing an essay rather than making calculations.

(*a*) *Read the question very carefully*, to ensure that you know precisely what is required. An answer to a question which has not been asked will earn no marks at all, even though it may be correct in every detail. Some questions are carefully phrased to assess the candidate's ability to think and to decide which points are involved.

(*b*) *Read the question a second time*, and prepare a rough list of the points that need to be covered. Only the briefest amount of detail is required, e.g. in the question above about documentary credits, the notes might be: definition of documentary credit, precise details on application form, confirmed, contract, revocable and irrevocable, examples of details, e.g. certificate of quality, etc.

(*c*) *Arrange the points in a logical sequence*. Thus, in the question above:

(*i*) definition of documentary credit;
(*ii*) revocable, irrevocable;
(*iii*) confirmed;
(*iv*) contract;
(*v*) precise details on application form;
(*vi*) examples of details, e.g. certificate of quality, etc.

It is essential to have your points in a logical order in this way, for the examiner can then see that you are capable of thinking out the answer and of writing a smooth-running essay with one point leading on to another. You may also avoid confusing and even contradicting yourself!

(*d*) *Write your answer in the form of an essay*, not in the form of numbered notes. There are some exceptions to the rule—where, for instance, you are required to list the risks covered by an ECGD policy—but usually such a question would go on to ask you to discuss some point or other (such as the advantages of credit insurance), when you should develop the answer in the form of an essay.

(*e*) *Use good phraseology and write neatly with a good pen.*

SPECIMEN QUESTION

What is meant by a forward exchange contract? In what circumstances might an importer enter into a forward option contract?

ROUGH NOTES

(1) Avoiding loss through exchange (2) rate fixed now, transaction later (3) some gain may be sacrificed (4) define option (5) option as to date only (6) uncertainty of date of payment (7) example.

MODEL ANSWER

Where an importer must make a payment in foreign currency at some date in the future, he will want to know how much the goods are going to cost him in terms of his own currency. Calculating at the current rate of exchange he may know that the goods will cost him £x, and therefore if he sells them at £x + y he will make a profit of £y. If in the meantime, however, the rate of exchange deteriorates he will receive fewer units of foreign currency for each unit of the home currency, and therefore the goods may cost him £x + y and his profit will disappear. A rather similar situation applies to the exporter who is to receive a certain amount of foreign currency in the future. He has based his price in the foreign currency on the current rate of exchange, but if in the meantime the value of the home currency appreciates he will receive fewer units of the home currency for each unit of foreign currency, and thus make a loss on his export.

Both the importer and the exporter can avoid the risk of loss by entering into a forward exchange contract. The importer can contract to buy the currency from his bank in, say, two months' time at a rate of exchange to be fixed immediately, while the exporter can enter into a contract to sell the currency at a future date at a rate to be fixed now. The bank, having bought currency forward, will sell it forward on the foreign exchange market; and if it has sold forward then it will buy the necessary currency forward through the market. It may be possible in effect for the bank to offset a forward purchase from one customer against a forward sale to another, and thus not require to cover itself through the foreign exchange market. In reality it will add together all its forward purchases and forward sales and buy or sell in the foreign exchange market only to the extent that it is necessary to make up the difference.

It is quite possible, of course, that the importer will find that the rate of exchange appreciates instead of depreciates, so that he would have been better off if he had bought the currency spot when it was actually required. Likewise, the exporter might find that the home currency depreciates instead of appreciates, but they cannot have it both ways. If there is any danger of loss then it is wise to avoid it if possible.

A forward option contract is one which gives the bank customer an option as to *when* he completes the transaction. It is not an option as to *whether* he completes the contract. When a trader is to make a payment in foreign currency or is to receive foreign currency in the near future and knows only approximately when, he can enter into an option contract which will give him a set period in which to complete the transaction. For instance, a three months' forward contract with option over the second and third months would be suitable when it is known that the currency will be required or paid at any time after a month but within three months.

An importer might enter into a forward option contract, therefore, when he knows that he has to pay for some goods in foreign currency in the near future, but is not sure of the exact date on which the currency will be required. He may, for instance, have contracted to pay for the goods one month after notification of shipment and be awaiting that notification. He knows that he will not have to pay for at least a month, but will for certain have to pay within the second month. He would therefore require a two months' forward contract with option over the second month.

2. Arithmetical questions. The following points should always be borne in mind in answering questions which involve calculations.

(*a*) *Read the question carefully*, to ascertain what calculations are required. Do not allow yourself to be misled by the fact that the question is very detailed. You must be able to decide quickly which of the details are relevant. If the question is concerned with the cost in sterling of purchasing some goods and/or the proceeds from selling goods, ask yourself, "What amounts of foreign currency are being bought (or sold) and when?"

(*b*) *Once you have decided on the calculations required*, the actual working out should be quite straightforward, especially as it is now normally permissible to use a calculator during an examination. But do work carefully or errors will occur which will lose you valuable marks.

(*c*) *Your calculations must be neat*, and it is advisable to show all your workings.

(*d*) *Work logically through the answer*, commenting on the steps that you are taking and why. The examiner can then see where you have gone wrong and give you marks for the right approach even though you do not succeed in arriving at the right answer. Refer to Questions 2–4 of Appendix VI for examples of how to set out your workings.

(*e*) *Always prepare a rough estimate* before embarking on a precise calculation. This will show you if your calculation is wide of the mark and cause you to stop and check instead of wasting time on completing a sum that is wrong near the beginning. It will also show you where the decimal point should be.

Specimen Test Papers

Do not attempt these papers until you have thoroughly mastered the relevant parts of the book, and the appropriate Progress Tests. Do each paper under strict examination conditions, bearing in mind the hints on exam technique given in Appendix IV. When you have completed a test, check your answer with the aid of text references.

Allow *three hours* for each paper; all questions carry equal marks. Answer *five* questions.

TEST PAPER 1

Foreign trade

1. What measures can be taken (*a*) to finance and (*b*) to rectify a balance of payments deficit?   (I, **10–16**)

2. Consider the ways in which a British bank can help an importer to pay for goods. Discuss the desirability of each of these methods from the point of view of the foreign supplier.   (II, **3–9**; IV, **1–2, 15–20**; V, **2, 4**)

3. Describe the main documents that are likely to be presented to a bank with a draft drawn under a documentary credit. What details in them would be given particular attention by the bank and why?   (V, **7–11**)

4. The *Uniform Customs and Practice for Documentary Credits* stipulates that credit instructions and the credits themselves must be complete and precise and that issuing banks should discourage any attempt by the applicant for the credit to include excessive detail.

Consider the reasons for the stipulation, and comment on the details that a bank requires on its application form for a documentary credit. (V, **12–13**)

5. In what ways is a back-to-back documentary credit similar to, and different from, a transferable credit?   (V, **17–20**)

6. How can an importer of goods protect himself when opening a documentary credit, bearing in mind that those handling the credit will be concerned with documents and not with the goods themselves?   (V, **7–13**)

7. When a bank collects or negotiates a documentary bill of

exchange it must obtain clear instructions from its customer. What points should be covered by such instructions?   (IV, **22** and Appendix III)

TEST PAPER 2

The foreign exchange market

1. What is meant by a forward exchange contract? When is a forward contract likely to be of use to a British importer?   (VIII, **1**)

2. Explain the terms "premium" and "discount" in connection with forward exchange and state what is meant by an option. From the following quotations calculate the rate at which a bank would buy francs at three months forward, option over the third month, and also the rate at which it would sell francs at one month forward fixed.

	French francs
Spot	$13.09\frac{1}{4}$–$10\frac{1}{4}$
One month forward	4–$3\frac{1}{2}$ c. pm
Two months forward	7–$6\frac{1}{2}$ c. pm
Three months forward	10–$9\frac{1}{4}$ c. pm (VIII, **5–7**)

3. On 1st November a London merchant signs a contract to buy 1,000 cases of tinned meat from Chicago at $49.50 per case for shipment during November and December. Payment is to be made immediately upon notification of shipment.

He further contracts, on the same day, to sell the tinned meat to a Belgian importer at 2,730 francs per case, and the shipment is to be sent direct to Antwerp c.i.f. by the American supplier. Payment is to be made one month after the date of shipment.

The London merchant arranges forward cover immediately for both transactions.

Exchange rates on 1st November are:

	US dollars	*Belgian francs*
Spot	2.6117–2.6127	114.60–114.75
One month forward	0.15–0.05 c. pm	40–30 c. pm
Two months forward	0.22–0.12 c. pm	70–60 c. pm
Three months forward	0.28–0.18 c. pm	100–90 c. pm

Exchange commission is 1 per mille with a maximum of £10.

Calculate the profit of the London merchant.   (VIII, **5–7**); X, pp. 82–8).

4. Put into your own words the following extracts from *The Financial Times*:

(*a*) Sterling rose 8 points against the US dollar to just over $2.6274 ... the pound was helped by the slackening in demand for dollars.

(*b*) There was no sign of any substantial Bank of England support in spot dealings, although the forward pound appeared to benefit from official operations.

(*c*) The German mark maintained its soft tone. Spot gains were made in terms of most Continentals, but not Dutch guilders.   (VII, **12**)

5. What factors determine the rate of exchange between two currencies? Why is it that speculation against the pound tends to be reflected more in forward rates than in spot rates?   (VI, **1–2**; VIII, **9–10**).

6. What are Euro-currencies? Why might a bank want to convert some of its Euro-currency deposits into its own currency?   (IX, **1–5**).

TEST PAPER 3

Development of overseas trade

1. Describe the methods whereby a British exporter of capital goods over three years may protect himself against the risk of non-payment. (XIII, **19–28**)

2. Describe the ways in which a London bank could assist an exporter of consumer goods.   (XI, **1–3, 7–14**)

3. What is meant by long-term export finance? Comment on recent developments in the provision of this type of finance.   (XI, **15–18**)

4. Briefly describe the main types of ECGD policy available to the exporter and comment on the risks covered by them.   (XIII, **8–29**)

5. In addition to the merchant and clearing banks there are a number of other institutions that offer services to the exporter. Comment on some of these and describe the services they provide.   (XII, **1–7**)

6. What is meant by post-shipment finance? Comment on the role of the British banking system in the provision of this type of finance. (XI, **13–18**)

Answers to Progress Test 10

(EXCHANGE ARITHMETIC QUESTIONS)

1. (a) 0.75   (d) 0.625
   (b) 0.375   (e) 0.125
   (c) 0.25   (f) 0.875

2. (a) *Answer* £1.13

$$\text{Rough estimate } \frac{£730 \times 5 \times 10}{100 \times 365} + 10\% = 1 + 10\%$$

$$= £1.1$$

$$\frac{749.12 \times 11 \times 5}{100 \times 365} = \frac{412,016}{365}$$

= 11,288
= £1.13

(b) *Answer* £71.07

$$\text{Rough estimate } \frac{£30,000 \times 12 \times 7}{100 \times 360} = £70$$

$$\frac{30,881 \times 12 \times 7}{100 \times 365} = \frac{2,594,004}{365}$$

= 71,068
= £71.07

(c) *Answer* £315.61

$$\text{Rough estimate} \quad \frac{£40,000 \times 72 \times 4}{365 \times 100} = £320$$

$$\frac{40,000 \times 72 \times 4}{365 \times 100} = \frac{1,152}{365}$$

= 315,616
= £315.61

(d) *Answer* $4.21

$$\text{Rough estimate} \quad \frac{400 \times 80 \times 5}{365 \times 100} = \frac{320}{73} = \$4.4$$

$$\frac{375.2 \times 82 \times 5}{365 \times 100} = \frac{153,832}{365}$$

= 42145
= $4.21

3. *Answer* £2,568.04

Two payments in dollars are to be made, one for $16,000 during September (one month forward option at $2.6102), and the other for $11,500 during September–October (two months forward option over two months at $2.6072).

$$\text{Rough estimate} \quad \frac{16,000}{2.5} = £6,400$$

$$\frac{11,500}{2.5} = £4,600$$

$$26,102 \overline{)16,000} \quad \frac{6,129.798}{}$$

= £6,129.80 *plus* exchange commission £6.13
                        = £6,135.93

$$\frac{4,410.862}{26,072\overline{)11,500}}$$

= £4,410.86 *plus* exchange commission £4.41

= £4,415.27

64,000 guilders will be received during October (one month after shipment) the forward rate applicable is therefore two months forward, option over the second month, therefore $8.37\frac{5}{8}$.

46,000 guilders will be received during October–November. Therefore the rate is three months forward, option over second and third month = $8.37\frac{5}{8}$.

NOTE: In both cases the dealer will *buy high* and therefore deduct the smallest premium possible which happens to be that for one month forward in both cases.

Rough estimates $\dfrac{64,000}{8}$ = £8,000

$\dfrac{46,000}{8}$ = £5,750

$$\frac{7,640.65}{837,625\overline{)64,000}}$$

= £7,640.65 *less* exchange commission £7.64

= £7,633.01

$$\frac{5,491.717}{837,625\overline{)46,000}}$$

= £5,491.72 *less* exchange commission £5.49

= £5,486.23

Credits	Debits
£7,633.01	£6,135.93
£5,486.23	£4,415.27
£13,119.24	£10,551.20
£10,551.20	

2,568.04 profit

4. *Answer* £1,571.03, £4,716.75
        £3,933.68, £627.93

NOTE: The significance of the actual dates of shipment is that they show that the forward contracts will provide the currency required, e.g. $12,150 bought two months forward will be taken up on 1st March, the last day of the option period. The actual shipments also show the amount of the excess shipment.

Payments to be made are as follows:
   (*i*) 1,000 × $4.05 at one month forward option (rate is $2.5805).
   (*ii*) 3,000 × $4.05 at two months forward, option over two months (rate is $2.5785).
   (*iii*) 2,500 × $4.05 at three months forward, option over second and third months (rate is $2.5765).
   (*iv*) 400 × $4.05 at spot 31st March (rate is $2.5825).

Rough estimates   (*i*) $$\frac{\$4,050}{2.5} = £1,620$$

                     (*ii*) $$\frac{\$12,150}{2.5} = £4,860$$

                     (*iii*) $$\frac{\$10,125}{2.5} = £4,050$$

                     (*iv*) $$\frac{\$1,620}{2.5} = £648$$

(*i*)
$$25,805 \overline{)4,050} \quad 1,569.46$$

= £1,569.46 *plus* exchange commission £1.57
                = £1,571.03
(*ii*)
$$25,785 \overline{)12,150} \quad 4,712.041$$

= £4,712.04 *plus* exchange commission £4.71
                = £4,716.75

(*iii*)
$$25,765 \overline{)10,125} \quad 3,929.75$$

= £3,929.75 *plus* exchange commission £3.93
= £3,933.68

(*iv*)
$$25,825 \overline{)1,620} \quad 627.299$$

= £627.30 *plus* exchange commission £0.63
= £627.93

Further Reading

The attention of students of banking, exporting and related areas is drawn to the following list of books published by the International Chamber of Commerce. They are available from the ICC at 38, Cours Albert ler, 75008 Paris, or from the British National Committee of the ICC at Centre Point, 103 New Oxford Street, London WC1A 1QB (telephone 01 240 5558). The publication number is given after each title; prices are available from the ICC on request.

The Problem of Clean Bills of Lading (283)
Standard Forms for Issuing Documentary Credits (323)
Guide to Documentary Credit Operations (305)
Decisions of the ICC Banking Commission (371)
Uniform Rules for a Combined Transport Document (298)
Uniform Rules for Contract Guarantees (325)
INCOTERMS (350)
Guide to INCOTERMS (includes INCOTERMS) (354)
Documentary Credits 1974 Rules and 1983 Rules compared and explained (411)
Key Words on International Trade (373)

Index